AUCTION READY

HOW TO BUY PROPERTY AT AUCTION EVEN THOUGH YOU'RE SCARED S#!TLESS

VERONICA MORGAN

i.e.

ind*i.e.* —
experts
IN OTHER WORDS

First published 2019 by Indie Experts
PO Box 1638, Carindale
Queensland 4152 Australia
indieexperts.com.au

Cover design by Jaimee Maree @ www.jaimeemaree.com
Edited by Samantha Sainsbury
Internal design by Indie Experts
Typeset in 10.25/15 pt Acumin Pro by Post Pre-press Group, Brisbane

A catalogue record for this book is available from the National Library of Australia

ISBN 978-0-6486736-0-6 (paperback)
ISBN 978-0-6486736-1-3 (epub)
ISBN 978-0-6486736-2-0 (kindle)

Disclaimer:
The material in this book is provided for information purposes only. The experiences discussed in this book may not necessarily be the same as the reader's experience. The reader should consult with his or her personal legal, financial and other advisors before utilising the information contained in this book. The author and the publisher assume no responsibility for any damages or losses incurred during or as a result of following this information.

CONTENTS

PROLOGUE   vii

INTRODUCTION   1

Buying property in Australia:

    The history of home ownership in Oz   2

How to get yourself ready for auction: About this book   5

CHAPTER 1 - WHO IS BUYING   9

Buyer profiles   10

CHAPTER 2 - WHAT PROPERTY TO BUY   33

Golden principles of buying property   34

CHAPTER 3 - THE GROUNDWORK:

MASTER THE MONEY SIDE OF PROPERTY   37

The deposit   37

Lenders mortgage insurance (LMI)   38

Stamp duty   40

Bank fees   41

Due diligence costs: legal fees & building/pest inspections   41

Council and water rates   42

Buyer's agents   42

Finance approval   44

Forming your A-team of property experts and specialists   49

Managing your expectations ahead of commencing your
    property search   51
Do your research to find a property   54
What are you committing to?   68

CHAPTER 4 - WHAT'S THE PROPERTY WORTH?   69
Demystifying real estate agent price guides   69
How to accurately calculate what the property is worth   78
How to set your maximum bid   84

CHAPTER 5 - DUE DILIGENCE   89
Buyer beware: Why you need to do due diligence
    and to have understood it   89
Avoid buying a lemon: What due diligence do you need to do?   90

CHAPTER 6 - BEFORE AUCTION:
BUYING BEFORE AUCTION DAY   103
Know your negotiation options   103
Pre-auction offers   105
Why, when and how real estate agents try to get you
    to make an offer before auction   118

CHAPTER 7 - AUCTION DAY:
BUYING PROPERTY AT AUCTION   123
Get prepared and give yourself a strategic advantage   123
The psychology of real estate auctions   126
The reserve price, vendor bids and when it is 'on the market'   133

CHAPTER 8 - BIDDING AT AUCTION   137
Bidding tactics for a winning strategy   137
Understanding your opponents: The different types
    of bidders   144
Your gameplan: What do you do when ...?   150
Sneaky tactics the auctioneer will use to get you to bid more   154
Bidder mistakes to avoid   157

CHAPTER 9 - AFTER THE AUCTION   159

Success! The property is yours   159

What happens if it passed in?   160

Buyers beware: The most vulnerable buyer is the one
who just missed out at auction   161

Getting back on the horse   163

GLOSSARY   165

ABOUT THE AUTHOR   169

PROLOGUE

It's almost ten a.m. on a Saturday and the auction is about to start. You adjust your sunglasses in the morning glare and scull the last dregs of the free coffee from the coffee cart that's now closing up shop. You've got a blinding headache from one too many reds last night. Glancing at your partner, you can see their lips are set in a firm line. They're just as hungover as you and not happy to be here. You're both still smarting from the disappointment of missing out on your dream house the previous week. Clinging to your leg, your youngest child starts whining about Peppa Pig. The babysitter cancelled at the last minute but rather than not attend you decided to pack everyone into the car anyway. The murmuring crowd falls silent as the auctioneer takes up his position, rolled-up contract in hand. As he begins his spiel, you start to sweat and feel your partner tense beside you. It's been a tough few months and you're both exhausted. This house isn't what you imagined buying when you started the process but you're here now, you paid for the building and pest inspection, the conveyancer and you registered to bid. You feel like the agents are watching you, willing you to put your hand up. Your daughter tightens her grip and her voice goes up an octave. Your partner bundles the child off to the side, away from the auction.

The auctioneer suggests a number right at the top of your price range and the number rings in your ears, making you question the more reasonable figure you had been imagining. Someone on your left raises their hand and confidently announces a number even higher. They look calm, relaxed even. They're smiling. Suddenly you feel gripped by a fear of missing out. You raise your hand and say a number above your maximum. Your partner's head whips around and they try to motion towards you while keeping hold of your child but the damage is done. The auctioneer looks pleased. The confident person on your left doesn't respond. The auctioneer keeps fishing but no one else bites. You glance around. The auctioneer seems to be winding up. Surely someone else will chime in? But no, the gavel falls and the house is yours. The confident would-be buyer who backed out before your bid claps along with everyone else and then strolls off down the street without a care in the world. How were they so calm? Why did they back out? What do they know that I don't? Questions whiz through your mind but it's time to head inside and sign the contract ...

INTRODUCTION

Why buy a property? Why put yourself through all the deprivation of saving up a deposit? The heartache when you miss out on your dream home? The dejection you feel when you know you're going to have to move away from where you really want to live, or settle for a shoebox in order to stay within a 30-minute commute to work. Is it really worth it?

Before I attempt to answer this for you, try fast forwarding your life 40 years. Imagine retiring and not owning your own home. Imagine living on the pension and having to pay rent. And if you're a self-funded retiree, imagine having to pay rent every week out of your diminishing superannuation. Imagine having to move in with your kids and losing your independence.

Sounds dramatic, but if you get a firm footing on the property ladder when you are young, you will have a much more comfortable life than you will if you don't. Of course, that doesn't mean that buying just any old property will do, but that's a topic for my next book. For now, keep reading, for I have a few tips coming up to help you avoid costly mistakes.

Property can be a very good investment for two reasons: compound growth and leverage. Compound growth means that the value grows exponentially – like a snowball gets bigger and bigger as it rolls down a hill. A good property in a good location will, over time, make you more money than you can save. When you add leverage (a financial term for borrowing money) you have more skin in the game – like having a bigger snowball in the first place – there's more surface area and it grows even faster as it gets bigger.

In Australia you also have a great tax advantage in owning and living in your own home. That increase in value – called capital growth – is tax free. When you sell, you get to keep it all, which will be particularly handy when you want to upgrade.

The advantages of buying a home are more than simply financial, they are emotional and psychological. For me, owning my own home gives me a sense of stability, of place, of security. It gives our kids somewhere to bed down memories, establish traditions; a place where they belong. We can decorate the way we want, hang pictures, paint, dig up the garden, install solar panels ... And when we make smart decisions we accumulate wealth in our homes and, over time, this equity gives us options and freedom.

So if you are looking to make the leap, invest your money wisely and put down roots, buying a house is the best way forward.

BUYING PROPERTY IN AUSTRALIA: THE HISTORY OF HOME OWNERSHIP IN OZ

The Great Australian Dream is alive and well, but it has changed over the past few decades and I believe it's on the cusp of changing again. That said, there is a vast array of property in this country and one person's castle is another's prison.

For instance, I live in the inner city. I can't imagine not being able to walk everywhere and have every convenience on my doorstep. My brother, on the other hand, hates traffic and crowds (not that I love them). He headed to the country as soon as he could and avoids coming into the city like the plague. Neither of us enjoyed living in suburbia, yet the vast majority of Sydneysiders would beg to differ. Our sister, on the other hand, left Australia altogether and is raising her young boys in an apartment in a historic town in Italy.

We Australians believe in our indelible right to own our own home and much has been made of this in popular culture – ever seen that classic film *The Castle* or the more kitchy *Emoh Ruo*?

My parents are Baby Boomers and they strived to own a quarter-acre block in suburbia. We grew up in a street with similar style houses, all built in the sixties and seventies. We spent our childhood outdoors in huge backyards (if you were really lucky, you had an above-ground pool) and playing footy with the neighbour's kids on the nature strip.

In the eighties the subdivisions continued and urban sprawl began overtaking the food bowls in the outskirts of our cities. The blocks were getting smaller; the houses growing larger. Kids spent more time indoors watching colour TV and playing 'Space Invaders'. It's even worse now with personal devices! In the cities, from where all the suburbanites had fled in the fifties and sixties, the process of gentrification began as some people started to value a shorter commute and the period charm of Victorian terraces and workers cottages.

Land in our ever-expanding cities seems to be in endless supply (did you know that Melbourne is now 100 kilometres wide?) and new suburbs with never-before-heard-of names entice first-home buyers with their shiny house and land packages. In the meantime, house prices in the inner rings of our cities have climbed to stratospheric heights because land is scarce.

Affordability is the word on everybody's lips, especially our politicians. Most of them are only referring to first-home buyers, but in reality the issue extends to renters too. The purpose of this book is not to discuss (nor pose solutions to) the 'affordability crisis' but we do need to acknowledge that it's there. It's another reason to buy your own home if you can – because in future decades more and more people will be priced out of home ownership in our cities. You will ensure your financial future if you buy well now.

This challenge will change the way we live, in fact it already has. Families are starting to embrace apartment living and a handful of enlightened developers are catering for multigenerational living. If we look to global cities like New York, London, Hong Kong, Milan, Paris, the majority of parents rear their children (and often a dog) in an apartment. In my view, it's the way of the future for our cities too. I just wish we also constructed buildings designed to last hundreds of years. Once again, this is a topic for another book.

One thing an apartment offers is more flexibility. They are easier to lock up and leave, they don't need as much maintenance as a house, they are easier to rent out (if they are in the right location, of course) and generally you get a better yield (higher ratio of rent to property value). Millennials tell me they don't want to be tied down by a home; they want to be free to relocate and work anywhere in the world. Owning an apartment can facilitate this more than a house can.

I'm Gen X, so if you're a Gen Y reading this, I hope you don't blame me if you feel you can't afford a home. You've probably heard this before, but we had our challenges too. Interest rates were ridiculously high. So, we could save a deposit easily enough but we could barely afford to repay the mortgage when we got it! I know your biggest challenge is to save the deposit (recent data shows that if you're single it will take you 12 years in Sydney and nine years in Melbourne to save enough to buy your first home). But once you do, the worst is over and you'll never have to save like that again (as long as you don't waste it – more on that later). It's worth the sacrifices: stay living with your parents, take a second job, be frugal, don't spend $60,000 on your wedding, travel later ...

Of course, if you don't live in Sydney or Melbourne, or possibly Brisbane, you won't be facing these challenges to the same extent, so count your lucky stars! You're also less likely to be buying at auction (by virtue of fewer of them being held in other areas) so I guess you probably aren't even reading this book. The market will always be changing and the economic climate with it. We can't know the future challenges our children will face, but with the right insights, you can overcome the challenges of today to achieve your dream of owning your own home. It's never an easy feat, just like generations past, but rest assured – it can be done!

HOW TO GET YOURSELF READY FOR AUCTION: ABOUT THIS BOOK

FEAR OF AUCTIONS

For many people, an auction combines several of the most stressful things in life all in one short interval: public speaking, complicated decision-making, the potential for 'losing' and the possible 'shame' of not succeeding. But it's worth considering how much a fear of auctions could really cost you.

WHY DO BUYERS HATE AUCTIONS?

Fear. Pretty much every objection a buyer has to going to auction has its origins in fear.

We fear the pain of missing out on a property we want. Auctions are conducted in a public arena. If you hate being the centre of attention, you'll be petrified at the thought of bidding in front of a crowd. None of us want to appear stupid and many buyers worry about getting caught up in a bidding war and paying a foolish price. Put simply, we don't feel like we're in control and that's very uncomfortable for most of us.

ARE THERE ANY BENEFITS FOR BUYERS?

Most buyers worry that in an auction the odds are stacked against them. Without the knowledge you'll gain from reading this book, this is a reasonable concern. However there are some very real benefits for buyers in the auction process.

The biggest benefit for property buyers is that of transparency. You can see your opponents. You can watch them and you know what they've just bid. In some states you can even watch them register to bid prior to the auction commencing. You don't get this level of transparency when negotiating outside the auction arena.

When the hammer falls, assuming the highest bid has met or exceeded the reserve price (more about this later), the highest bidder is the buyer. The deal is done and there is no risk of being gazumped.

DO YOU WANT TO RESTRICT YOUR PROPERTY OPTIONS?

Some buyers fear auctions so much that they never look at a property unless it has an asking price. Unfortunately, though, avoiding auctions in some areas means you are limited to the dregs as the vast majority of quality property is marketed for auction. In Sydney's inner ring nearly everything is offered for sale by auction and it's a similar situation in Melbourne. Even in Brisbane and Adelaide, where the auction culture is not as strong, you'll find that many of the more desirable houses are auctioned. Unless you want to buy the leftovers, you'll need to get comfortable with the auction process. Keep reading, because that's what this book will help you do!

FEAR CAN ENCOURAGE YOU TO MAKE UNWISE PRE-AUCTION OFFERS.

In chapter 6 we go into a lot of detail about making pre-auction offers. There are times when they are warranted, however many people make them purely out of fear of going to auction. There are many mistakes that buyers make when making offers before auction and one of the biggest is paying too much. An unintended consequence can be the creation of a bidding war, and often the person who fires the first shot ends up losing the battle.

FEAR CAN CAUSE YOU TO CLAM UP WHEN YOU SHOULD BID

I've seen bidders paralysed at auction. They second-guess themselves or they are overwhelmed by a more confident bidder. They give up, even when they have more money to spend. They say, 'That person was going to keep on bidding anyway, so that's why I stopped.' Frankly, this is rubbish. They don't know what other buyers are thinking, nor do they know how much other buyers can afford. It's a mind game and they were the losers.

The only way to reduce your chances of either missing out or paying too much at auction is to be well prepared. The first step is to educate yourself about the market and keep up to date with recent sale prices.

Auctions are stressful and making significant, long-term decisions can be complicated and overwhelming. Throughout this book you will find strategies to help you overcome flawed thinking and bamboozling emotions in order to make smart, informed, logical decisions to achieve your goals. Having awareness is a good first step, but it's important to have strategies to keep you focussed on rational decision-making and thought processes.

Auction Ready will do exactly what it says: get you ready for auction so that you will know exactly what to do in order to buy that property. So settle in and let's get started.

CHAPTER 1

WHO IS BUYING

If you're reading this, chances are you've been out looking for a home. You may have even found one you want to bid for. You've been dealing with agents and you've been trying to work out which ones you can believe, how much you should pay and what research you need to do before you're actually ready to buy. You've probably been asking your parents for advice, your boss, your workmates and your mortgage broker. And if you're feeling nervous about it all, that's for good reason – not only is this a *big* decision, most of these people know only a little bit more than you do.

But let's wind back a bit. Unless you've won the lottery or come into an inheritance, you've probably made huge sacrifices in order to save a deposit. This money is precious and you do not want to waste it. If you already own a home and you're planning on upgrading, you've already done the hard yards. That's great, but you might also secretly admit to yourself that there was luck involved and you're not really sure you're doing it right this time around.

Buying a home is a little bit like getting married. You generally can't have more than one house at a time, so in choosing one you are making a commitment to forgo all others (at least for a while, the wonderful thing about property is that if you get it right, you can legally become a 'bigamist'). As we covered in the introduction, there are financial *and* emotional reasons for buying your own home and the consequences of getting it wrong will impact both areas of your life. You want to avoid that.

Contrary to popular belief, the biggest mistake you can make isn't paying too much (although you can avoid that if you take my free short course: www.getauctionready.com.au/bonus); it's *buying the wrong property*. It is possible to lose money in property if you buy something that is poorly located or lacks scarcity. You can also lose by buying the wrong home for your needs and then having to sell too quickly. A lot of money is lost in paying additional stamp duty and agent's fees.

I personally think that the emotional cost of making a poor choice is much more long lasting than the financial cost. Living with regret if you make the wrong decision is pretty horrible, especially when the stakes are so high. Wrong decisions come from fear, tunnel vision, poor advice, simply not knowing what you don't know. That's why I've written this book, to help you avoid those mistakes.

BUYER PROFILES

FIRST-HOME BUYERS

In my career I've met first-home buyers ranging from single professionals with high incomes to double-income couples in their thirties with small kids, through to older singles in their fifties who just came into an inheritance! One thing that unites them all is a feeling of excitement tinged with (often extreme) nerves.

The property you buy for your first home is most likely to be a 'stepping stone' home. That is, it won't be your first and last. Choosing wisely now will give you greater choice when it comes to your next move. There are a number of options available for first-home buyers and the right one for you will depend on your circumstances. Here are some that many first-home buyers consider.

One-bedroom apartments

Well-located one-bedroom units can be good investments but they don't offer much flexibility for owner-occupiers.

This is not a great option if you think you'll live in it and will outgrow it quickly (in less than five years). It also won't work if you need the flexibility of being able to rent out a second bedroom in order to help with the mortgage at any stage.

A one-bedroom apartment can be a great option for those who intend to stay single, or if you travel a lot and want to use this as a city pad, or if you expect your income to substantially increase in future years and this will be kept as an investment property. If the latter applies to you, make sure you talk to an accountant and an investment-savvy mortgage broker who will ensure you structure your loan to maximise any future tax savings.

House and land packages

House and land packages in new subdivisions on the outskirts of our cities are heavily marketed to first-home buyers.

I have one piece of advice for you: don't do it. Of course, shiny and new is appealing but there are issues when it comes to short- and long-term capital growth. I know you think you'll live in it forever, but what if you get an interstate job transfer, or (God forbid) you get divorced and you have to sell sooner rather than later? You can easily lose money.

Why? Because property prices go up as a result of supply and demand. Once that subdivision is sold, there's usually a new suburb created right next door. Which means newer houses than yours to tempt new buyers. A new house is like a brand new car, it loses money the minute you drive it out of the showroom.

The actual value is in the land, not the house. As our cities expand, the blocks of land get smaller and smaller, which has an impact on the value of the asset over time.

I could write an entire book on this topic but for now I'll stop on one last point. These new subdivisions often have very poor infrastructure, which means public transport is either non-existent or overcrowded. You will be reliant on two cars and your commute could be punishing. Enough said.

Off-the-plan apartments

These are also promoted to first-home buyers and seem like a good option because you don't need to have the entire deposit saved up when you commit to the purchase.

Just as with house and land packages, brand-new apartments often lose money the minute you turn the key in the front door. The risks with buying off-the-plan and brand-new apartments extend even further as you have no control over the build quality. Statistics indicate over 70 percent of all new buildings have defects, so you and all your neighbours could be carrying the can for these for years. It's not worth the risk.

Renovator's delights

A great opportunity to add value quickly to a property is through renovating, although not all renovation potential is equal and not all would-be renovators are up to the challenge.

Putting in a new kitchen and bathroom, painting and polishing floorboards is the easiest type of renovation. There is nothing structural about these changes, no additions required, no council applications, no architects. These sorts of changes can be a great way to improve a property as long as all the rooms are in the right spot in the first place.

If the property requires more extensive renovations, you'll need to be honest about your capabilities, your access to more money (get advice on how much you'll need *before* you buy) and whether the property actually deserves to be renovated (does it have good bones?). You don't want to overcapitalise (that is, spend more money than it ends up being worth) and you equally don't want to get stuck with a lemon you can't afford to fix.

Knock down and rebuilds

This is different to buying a house and land package. In more established suburbs where the homes are 40–50 years old you'll often see a wave of new owners coming in, knocking down the old, modest homes and building much larger, modern homes.

This can be an effective strategy for first-home buyers who can live comfortably in the original home for some years before they can access the funds to rebuild. It works well if you know and love the area, because it's a long-term play. You'll also need to know that you'll have access to the additional funds when you're ready to upgrade.

Rentvesting

This is an option for first-home buyers who can't afford to buy a home where they want to live. The idea is that they rent where they live and buy where they can afford. It might be that they live in a very expensive area and need to buy somewhere else entirely. Or it may be that they can't afford a large enough property in their area. This way they can still get onto the property ladder even though they technically can't afford their own home.

The thing to be mindful of is buying an investment-grade property. That is, one with strong potential for capital growth. There's more on this further on in this chapter.

FAQs

Q: How do I avoid getting outwitted by agents?

A: Arm yourself with research. And by that I mean inspect, inspect, inspect and keep track of sale prices. Start inspecting before your finance is approved so that you are an educated buyer. Never make an offer before you've done your price research (here's the link to my free course that will teach you how to do this: www.getauctionready.com.au/bonus) and when you are clear on price, the agent will be less able to call your bluff by talking about other 'higher offers'.

Q: Should I buy off my parents?

A: This all depends on whether you want to live in that house in that location, whether your siblings will be put out (family and money rarely play well) and whether your parents are offering it to you to help you, or whether you are making them an offer. Personally, I'd steer clear of this – go out and forge your own path.

Q: Is a big deposit best?

A: Usually it is. If you have a 20 percent deposit you will avoid paying lenders mortgage insurance (LMI) and you will start off in a more secure position because you'll have more equity from day one. Although, there are some exceptions to this rule.

If you are buying an inferior property at a lesser price than you can afford just so you can avoid LMI, you could be making a poor long-term decision. For example, if you are buying on a main road to save money but you could afford a home in a quiet street, I'd recommend having a smaller deposit and a quieter home. Long term your home will grow in value faster than one on a busy road.

Another example is if you are buying a small home that you will outgrow quickly. The costs of upgrading in a short period of time will outweigh the benefits of having started with a larger deposit.

In a rising market, where property prices go up faster than you can save, getting in quickly with a smaller deposit might serve you best. In a flat or falling market, you can take more time to save up more.

Lenders mortgage insurance (LMI)

This is something you have to pay if your deposit is less than 20 percent. Some banks offer professionals (doctors, lawyers, accountants) the opportunity to avoid LMI as long as they have a 10 percent deposit. The important thing to understand is that this insurance does not protect you, the borrower. It protects the bank in the event that you can't pay the mortgage.

There is such a thing as borrowers mortgage insurance, which is an additional cost but well worth looking into. Ask your broker about this.

Government grants

I've got one piece of advice for all first-home buyers – forget government grants. They are more likely to do you harm than good. They are not a good reason to buy and if you happen to qualify, take it as icing on the cake.

Why do I say this? Because they are a temptation that can lead first-home buyers into the trap of buying a poor-quality property. Often they only apply if you buy brand new (see below for why these are the *riskiest* properties you can buy) or you have to spend under a set price limit in order to qualify.

It's a mistake for first-home buyers to spend under $650,000 (that's the limit in NSW) just in order to get a government grant if they could afford to spend more and therefore get a better property. In NSW you'll save up to $25,000 in stamp duty but in order to stay under the threshold you might either buy something that's too small or not where you really want to live. If it's too small, you'll outgrow it quickly and need to upgrade. Then what? You sell and buy the bigger home you should have bought in the first place? In doing so, you incur selling costs and end up paying stamp duty any way. You could easily be out of pocket to the tune of $100,000 within a few short years. Under this scenario your initial stamp-duty saving has ended up costing you $75,000.

What if you bought where you really don't want to live and after a while decide to move elsewhere? Could you keep this property as an investment? Maybe, but it will limit your options. You may find you can't borrow enough to buy in your ideal suburb and will need to return to renting. If your goal was to buy and live in your own home, you're back to square one.

Forget short-term incentives that limit what you buy. Buy the best property you can afford in the best location you can afford. Keep your eye firmly on the big picture and you'll make better decisions.

Common mistakes by first-time buyers

All property is NOT equal

You'll often hear advice that any property will do, just get onto the ladder. It's an underlying belief that many Aussies have: that we should all own a property and we haven't really made it until we do. And yet, without questioning this belief, without realising that all property is not equal, many people blindly buy as soon as they're able to, without taking a moment to check whether it's a good idea. This goes for owner-occupiers and investors. Think of the first-home buyers who queued in order to buy a one-bedroom unit off-the-plan because they thought it was the quickest way to get on the ladder. Many of them will be stuck on that rung of the ladder for a very long time.

Looking to your mortgage broker for advice beyond the finance

Don't get me wrong, I love mortgage brokers and I recommend all of our clients use them. Mortgage brokers and bank-lending managers tell me that buyers often ask them what they should pay for a property. Most then give the buyer an automated valuation (AVM), which many banks provide. If you then went out and got nine more AVMs from similar institutions, you'd get 10 different suggested selling prices and an incredibly unhelpful spread of possible values. I have numerous case studies that illustrate this. Brokers and lenders think they're being helpful, but this is actually very dangerous for the buyers they're trying to help. If you're given an AVM, don't look at the recommended price, in fact cross it out so you're not swayed by it. Many of them are too high, especially when the market is falling. Instead, look at the recent sales and start assessing for yourself how they compare to the property you want to buy. I have a *free* mini course that will show you how to do this and avoid overpaying: www.getauctionready.com.au/bonus.

Brand new does not mean perfect

Buying a brand-new property is highly risky, especially apartments in large complexes. There are building issues that often come up, water penetration is the most common and it's extremely expensive to fix. I've heard statistics suggesting as many as 73–97 percent of new buildings have defects. Even if the builder makes good, even if there is a warranty, you are still the person who has to live in a defective building. Or your tenants have to and they may choose to move out or demand a rent reduction. The drama around getting repairs identified, quoted, working out who is responsible and who will pay can take years, even extending into a second decade. The damage this causes is not limited to the property itself, but to our emotional and mental wellbeing. Another risk area is the design itself. If you're buying off-the-plan and you can't read plans, you're in dangerous territory. An apartment with a poorly designed floor plan can't be fixed. You can't renovate around it. You're stuck with it. When you go to sell, other buyers will be able to see in reality what you missed on a drawing.

Capital growth matters

'Capital growth is not my priority because it's our family home and we're going to live in it for 20 years.' I've lost count of the number of times I've heard this. It seems logical until you consider how they'll feel in 20 years' time when they are presented with the opportunity cost of that thinking. Growth rates vary significantly between locations and within locations, between individual properties. And the longer you hold them, the difference between high and low performers grows exponentially. To give an extreme example of locations, the median house price went up around 25 percent in Brisbane over the last 10 years while it went up 89 percent in Sydney over the same period. Theoretically, what this means is that if you spent $500,000 in each city 10 years ago, it's possible that the Brisbane home is now worth $625,000 and the Sydney house $1,134,000.* That's a difference of over half a million dollars. I have a specific case study on a house in Balmain that shows it tracked

---

* It's important to note that not every suburb within a city has the same median growth rate. For instance, over those ten years in Brisbane, some suburbs may have shown as little as 10 percent growth while others may have gone up 60 percent.

$178,000 *under* the median growth rate in the suburb over a 12-year period. After 20 years, when those people go to downsize, they'll find their options are limited because better-quality assets continue to grow at a higher rate than their home does. There's a good chance there'll be a bit of regret there, especially if they have friends who had made better original choices.

Entry-level homes can be traps

Buying on a main road in a premium area because that's the only way you can afford to be in that suburb is never a good idea. There are so many reasons this strategy is flawed. For starters, if you want the snob value of having that address, anybody in a better street will look at you as being the poor cousin. Main roads are uncomfortable to live on: they're noisy, dirty and it's often difficult to get in and out of your driveway. Insulation and double glazing can be effective, but not if you like to sleep with the windows open. As populations rise, traffic is only going to get worse and I wouldn't bet on electric cars being quieter. If ever you need to sell, you might struggle to find a buyer: in a soft market they won't even inspect because of the address. Capital growth over time will be less than the median for that suburb, so if you are able to upgrade at some future stage, it will probably cost you more than if you'd bought in a quiet street in a nearby suburb that wasn't so premium.

Self-imposed maximum budget

Now don't get me wrong, it's important to know how much you can afford to spend on a property. Yet I've met a lot of buyers in my time who set a more conservative limit than they needed to. It's fine to do this if the buyer is very aware of the market and exactly what is available in each price bracket but most aren't. Price brackets move around. At any given time in any given suburb there will be price points where there's a gap of buyers. Just above that gap there are properties that offer quite a bit more for not a huge amount more money. Say, for instance, there are a lot of buyers looking for unrenovated houses under $1M. These buyers don't have more money, and not nearly as many buyers have $1.1M. In this scenario a fully renovated house might sell for $1.15M whereas the cost to renovate might be $200,000. Limiting your budget and not noticing that there's a tipping point just above your range is a classic mistake.

Imagine if you can get a lot more for your money with only a slightly increased budget. It's worth checking out the properties just out of your reach just to make sure.

Ignoring a bad building inspection

We humans are strange beings. Sometimes we ask for advice and don't take it. Sometimes we even pay for that advice and still don't take it. Why is that? Buying a home is a very emotional process. It's more than just a roof over our head; it's status, security, a feeling of achievement, we can pat ourselves on the back for providing for our family ... If we want a particular property for more reasons than just the accommodation it provides, then maybe we're being driven by our subconscious and therefore biased when it comes to the due diligence. An example is confirmation bias – where we actively seek out information that supports the beliefs we already hold. We know we should do a building and pest inspection but we want it to be positive because we don't want to deviate from the path we've already started upon. This is called consistency bias. When the building inspection refers to some major issues, our subconscious is what leads us to gloss over these problems. Our rational minds would never do that, right? Of course, no building is perfect. Every inspection report will note something that needs attention. Just be realistic about the magnitude and budget accordingly.

UPGRADERS

When you've outgrown your home (maybe having a second or third child has tipped the balance, or your kids are in high school and it suddenly seems like the house is too small for all these adult-sized humans), you're going to be faced with the dilemma of whether to buy before you sell or vice versa.

There is no one-size-fits-all answer to this question, although there is one simple rule to follow: do whatever is hardest first. This usually comes down to how easy your home will be to sell.

Step one is to find out how much money your bank will lend you and whether you can borrow enough to cover owning two properties for a period of time. If they will give you bridging finance, make sure you understand the costs and whether there is a time limit. If you cannot fund more than one property at a time, the answer is clear: you need to sell before you can buy.

If your bank will lend you the funds, then you need to consider market conditions before deciding to buy before you sell. Does the market favour the buyer or the seller? Are you buying and selling in the same location? Or are you planning on an interstate move, or a tree/sea change? City and regional markets can differ substantially and getting the timing right (or wrong) will have a much greater impact on your financial position.

If you are moving out of a market where it will be easy to sell and into a market where it's difficult to find the perfect home, then I'd suggest that you buy before you sell. If, on the other hand, you have the type of home that has a limited buyer pool, you might be better off selling first.

In a buyers' market you will find it harder to sell than to buy, therefore selling first will usually be the best plan. The price you can expect to get for your current home will be less certain so you will find it difficult to know exactly what the budget should be for your new home. By selling first you will know precisely how much money you will have to spend and be able to turn the market conditions to your advantage as you can expect plenty of property on the market to choose from when you are ready to buy.

When in a sellers' market, it stands to reason that you are going to find it easier to sell, so in most cases it's better to buy before you sell. When you look to buy there will be a scarcity of property to choose from and fierce competition from other buyers. If you sell first, you run the risk of a long lead-time before securing your next property. You may also have to rent in between transactions. Many buyers in this situation find themselves tempted to make a panic purchase, which they could live to regret all too quickly.

In a sellers' market, there is another compelling reason to buy before you sell. When prices are rising, if you don't buy back in quickly, you run the risk of being priced out of the market.

In my business, one of the ways we guide our clients through the dilemma of whether to buy first or sell first is to help them gain clarity about exactly the sort of property they will be able to buy. Often people have unrealistic expectations, so it's important that they start from a position of knowledge. Even if you cannot get bridging finance and don't have the option to buy before you sell, knowing what and where to buy before you even list your property for sale will give you a distinct advantage. It will allow you to hit the ground running the moment you find a buyer for your place.

Using equity in your current house to buy something else

One of the benefits of working with an investment-savvy mortgage broker is that they will help you structure your loan in order to give you the maximum amount of flexibility for the future. For example, you could have been making use of an offset account and can access this money to pay the deposit on another property. Another facility your broker may have recommended is a line of credit. You may be able to use these funds to pay a deposit. Just remember that you'll be paying more interest the minute you take this money out of the bank. Of course you must ensure you have your finance approved to cover the balance on settlement day!

If you are upgrading your home and decide to buy before you sell, make sure that you have spoken to your broker and arranged bridging finance to cover you for both properties until you sell your current home.

What if you've sold your house already?

If you decide to sell before you buy, you'll still need to arrange access to money to pay a deposit in case you find a home before you settle on your old one. As I've mentioned above, an offset account or line of credit may solve that problem. If you don't have either of these facilities, your broker can discuss other options with you, such as a deposit bond or personal loan.

A word of caution

If you have decided to sell before you buy, you are susceptible to being pressured to buy immediately after selling. Most people resist the idea of renting after they've been a home owner and who wouldn't want to avoid a double move, after all?

It is at this time – when you're in buying mode, when your finances are ready, when you are at your most motivated to move and your fear of missing out is at its zenith – that you are most open to the lure of an available, often inadequate, piece of real estate.

Selling agents see you coming – they can smell the desperation, the panic and they rub their hands together in glee! You are not thinking clearly; you have momentarily forgotten your property checklist; you just want this nightmare to be over and to be settled again. And they see a chance to shift some stock that has been taking a while to sell ... No other buyer will be so blind to the shortcomings of this particular property.

Beware: this is the time you need to be more critical than ever! Try the helicopter approach and look at the big picture. Remember why you wanted to move in the first place and revisit your property requirements. Organise your checklist so that your 'must-haves' are at the top of the list. Remind yourself of what you are prepared to compromise on as you inspect the next property. Now be honest with yourself: are you buying out of fear or because this is the right property for you?

Repeat after me: there are worse things than renting. Buying the wrong property is much worse!

One last word, don't try to outsmart the market. Waiting for the peak to sell and the trough to buy is a mug's game. Not even the experts can pick these two points in the cycle, you'll only know for certain after the moment has passed. When buying a home, buy when you're ready.

DOWNSIZERS

Timing the sale and purchase for downsizing is much more critical for people in or approaching retirement because they have no runway to recover from mistakes. If they're still working, they may have only a few earning years left and so every dollar from the sale of their home counts in a different way.

Typically downsizers wait for a rising market as, in theory at least, the higher-value homes climb in value faster than smaller, cheaper homes. Sometimes this plays out very well, and selling and buying at the right time can top up the retiree's nest egg. However there are times when the 40-year-old family home simply doesn't appeal to today's young-family buyer.

Home owners who are no longer earning an income are less likely to be able to get bridging finance, so selling before buying will often be the best option. Needless to say, the prospect of being 'homeless' for any period of time will be daunting, so it's incredibly important to research the market and be very clear on the likely options for downsizing. Go to open houses and keep a track of sale prices so your expectations and budget are aligned.

FIRST-TIME INVESTORS

Most property investors in Australia stop at one property. Latest data has it at close to 70 percent. The main reason, I believe, is that their investments have failed to do what they were meant to. In my experience, only around five percent of property that is on the market at any given time is investment grade. Given this, it's easy to see why first-time investors get it wrong.

There are a number of options for residential-property investors (please note, I'm not going to cover commercial and industrial property in this book) and a lot of property spruikers and advisors sell very compelling 'systems' and 'strategies'. Property investment is a risky business and it's my view that you want to take the least amount of risk to make the greatest gain. First-time investors have one shot at this, so it's important that your one shot hits the bullseye. For this reason, I implore you to chase capital growth and *not* rental income. To find out eight reasons why, check out the bonus content on www.getauctionready.com.au/bonus. If you are after an income-producing asset, talk to a financial planner about other, less risky, options.

FAQs

Q: What makes an investment-grade property?

A: Location is number one. In Australia, in my view, the safest places to invest are the inner suburbs of Sydney and Melbourne. Of course, not everyone can afford investment-grade properties in these areas. Here are the four elements that underpin an investment-grade location.

1. High demand from owner-occupiers. Ideally you want to buy into an area where tenants make up around 30 percent of the inhabitants. You want enough tenants in order to ensure your place is always rented and you also want a lot of demand from owner-occupiers to ensure that there will be a buyer for you one day in many years' time when you finally sell.

2. Strong economy. These tenants and owner-occupiers need to earn their income from somewhere and we look for a number of solid employers in different market sectors. Mining towns and tourist hubs are notoriously bad locations to invest in because when their one and only industry hits a downturn, people lose their jobs and leave the town. (We also want to see buzzing town centres, investment in infrastructure, etc.)

3. Good incomes. Hand-in-hand with employers, we look for high-earning locals. This is the reason that inner Sydney and Melbourne do so well, the people who earn good salaries want to live there and will compete in order to buy a home with an easy commute and access to great lifestyle features such as beaches, cafes, shops, parks ...

4. Population growth. More people means more demand for housing, which is great for property investors!

The location on its own is not enough, however. Once you've identified a location, it's critical that you choose a property with characteristics that will make it more appealing to tenants and other buyers in the future. Some features are universal – northerly aspect, natural light, quiet street – and some will be specific to that location. Nothing beats local knowledge, so make sure you familiarise yourself with the type of property that attracts the widest range of buyers in that area.

Q: Why is capital growth more important than yield?

A: It's a principal of property investment that high yield (rental income) and strong capital growth (increasing values) are mutually exclusive. Yield comes with risk and I never encourage anybody to take unnecessary risks when buying property. If you need to have the rent entirely cover your mortgage repayments and you don't have a large deposit (please discuss this with your accountant), then I encourage you to also talk to a financial planner and consider other forms of investment.

Q: Should I buy in my self-managed super fund (SMSF)?

A: This was a bit of a craze a few years back and some accountants and property spruikers made a lot of money from convincing people with moderate super fund balances to set up a SMSF and buy a brand-new property. Many of those people now have less money in their super than they did when they started.

That's not to say everybody who invested in their super has made a mistake. I bought a nice solid red-brick apartment in mine and it's doing well. The issue today is that most of the banks have stopped lending to SMSFs and the handful that do charge much higher interest rates than they do for normal investment loans (we're talking around 50 percent more). As a result, buying property in your SMSF has lost its shine.

Common mistakes by first-time investors

Buying around the corner from your home

Of course, you know the area, you can drive past it and keep an eye on it, it's a great suburb, after all, you've already bought there, right? Not necessarily.

Apart from not diversifying, you're probably succumbing to home bias and taking the easy route. Buying an investment property needs a *lot* more investigation than that.

Chasing affordability

There are plenty of investors who bought in 'affordable' locations because they thought they 'should' have an investment property and then find it hardly goes up in value. Taking the time to get yourself in a position to buy a quality property for the long term is really the only safe way to go about it. Getting on the ladder at all costs is fraught with risk.

Hotspotting

Hotspotting is where you invest in the next suburb or area that's going to take off. The trouble is that a lot of these areas take off but then the cycle turns and they go down. If you don't get your timing absolutely spot on, you'll buy at the wrong time or sell at the wrong time or both.

If you are trying to ride the cycle, you are speculating, not investing. Even professionals fail at speculating, so my recommendation is don't do it. Property investment is a long game. If you buy a quality asset in a sound location and let it do its thing, in 10 years' time you'll see how a good investment pays off by being worth a *lot* more than you paid for it.

Not understanding cash flow

You are likely to have out-of-pocket expenses for at least the first five years of owning a good-quality investment property so it's important that you have factored this into your budgeting.

As a rough rule of thumb, take the rental income, minus 25 percent to cover costs such as property-management fees, insurance, maintenance, levies, etc. and then see how much extra you'll need to have available to cover the mortgage repayments.

Investing to reduce tax

Your accountant might suggest that you have a tax problem and need to buy an investment property to solve it. This is a bad reason to buy an investment property. Negative gearing is what they're talking about and in order to get tax back, you have to actually lose money.

The thing to understand is that the only reason you should be happy to lose money is because you are confident that the property is making money for you by growing in value. Of course, these gains aren't ever cash in your pocket (until you sell) but they will help you gain financial freedom as you head towards retirement.

The problem with investing to save tax is that people often invest in poor-quality assets. They get lured into buying brand-new apartments, for example, because they get loads of tax deductions. But what they don't realise is that an alarmingly high proportion of brand-new apartments lose money over the first 10 years of ownership. Now that's what I call a bad investment.

Of course, once you have bought an investment grade property, it will help with your cash flow to get a bit of tax back and I encourage you to get advice from your accountant and maximise your deductions.

GEN Y AND MILLENNIAL BUYERS

Pitfalls of getting help from parents

As well-meaning as they may be, your parents are rarely the best source of property advice. What worked for them won't necessarily work for you and many of them think that property ownership is a rite of passage into adulthood. I see all too often that parents overpay at auction when helping out their sons and daughters. Parents want the best for their kids and they hate to see them miss out but helping them overpay is not the best way to set them up financially.

If your parents offer you money, make sure it comes with no strings, or with a formal loan agreement if you're expected to repay them. If they offer to go guarantor so that you avoid paying lender's mortgage insurance, you all need to get some legal advice beforehand.

Friends can also be a dangerous source of advice because, like your parents, they are well meaning and you trust them. Yet property is a complex beast and even if they've had some personal successes, their circumstances and life goals may be very different to yours. Plus, they are likely to be heavily biased in favour of what they've decided to do and won't really understand the risks overall.

Negative equity

If you value freedom and flexibility, be very careful – some property will trap you!

Property is a long-term commitment. If you need to sell for some reason and can't cover your purchase price plus costs, you'll lose money. It's not commonly talked about but not every property actually increases in value over time. You really want to avoid negative equity.

Negative equity means you owe more money to the bank than the property is worth. If prices fall more than 10 percent and you bought with just a 10 percent deposit, you will have negative equity.

If you owe more than the property is worth you probably won't be able to afford to sell and upgrade in years to come when you need a larger home. Obviously, not all property is at risk of losing value, so care needs to be taken to understand what the danger signs are before you buy.

CHAPTER 2

WHAT PROPERTY TO BUY

I'm going out on a limb here: not all property is worth buying. The bottom line is that not all property makes a good investment in the pure sense. In fact, only a very small proportion of real estate is worth investing in if your end goal is financial freedom. If you are buying a place to live in, however, there are other benefits of home ownership that need to be taken into account. Security is a huge one!

There is a bit of soul searching I recommend you do when considering what to buy, such as:

1. Why you are buying?

2. What you need versus what you want

3. How long will it be before you need to upgrade?

4. What you can afford?

5. Where you are buying?

The entry and exit costs of buying property are very high, so it's important to try to minimise the amount of times you need to buy and sell over your lifetime. Think about what your needs are likely to be in five, 10, 15 years and consider whether your decisions are short term or long term.

GOLDEN PRINCIPLES OF BUYING PROPERTY

In every location there will be types of property that attract more competition than others. Take the time to learn about the characteristics that are popular with local buyers so that you can choose a property that will be more popular down the track when you come to sell it.

If you are buying a 'renovator's delight', make sure you speak to the local council about what is permitted and also get advice from an architect and/or builder. You'll also need to clarify how you are going to fund the renovations. Too many people get caught out by assuming they can make improvements that will never get approval.

Whether you are buying for investment or a home to live in, be careful to avoid locations where less than 70 percent of the property is owner occupied. Fundamentally, owner-occupiers provide market stability while overactive investors can create price volatility. That said, like every rule, there are exceptions, such as blue-chip, inner-city suburbs where the percentage of investors could be as high as 40 percent without posing a high risk. When it comes to our largest asset, we want to avoid volatile markets. The major internet real-estate portals have suburb data where you access this information.

If you are buying an investment property, please be very careful about buying for yield. I firmly believe that capital growth is the primary goal of any real-estate investment. Tying up a lot of equity or borrowing capacity on a property that doesn't grow in value or has minimal growth is foolish.

One thing to always be mindful of is supply and demand. This is particularly important if you are looking to buy an apartment or house in a new subdivision. If there are hundreds (or even thousands) of apartments being built nearby, steer clear. If you are buying in a new subdivision and there are plans in place for more and more new land releases nearby, think again. The problem is a lack of scarcity. When all the properties are similar, future buyers have choice and price growth will be hampered as a result. Even worse, when you have more and more new properties released, the ones that are only a few years old start to look very tired in comparison.

I am not a fan of brand-new or off-the-plan apartments. A lack of scarcity and potential for oversupply are not the only problems. There are enormous risks when it comes to build quality and, until governments provide greater protection for consumers, my advice is to prioritise apartments that are at least 15 years old.

Most apartments are strata title, which means that you effectively own the airspace within the external walls, floor and ceiling of your lot. You will pay quarterly levies that cover such things as building insurance and your contribution to the maintenance of common property, which includes the roof, windows, foyers, lifts, gardens, gym, pool, etc. In larger complexes there may be a number of different strata titles and a community title that covers the shared facilities.

Less common are company title apartments, which are likely to be Art Deco buildings located in the inner city. When you own one of these units, you effectively own shares in the company and the right to occupy your lot. The banks don't like to lend money for these because they aren't what is technically referred to as 'real property.' Some buildings have very restrictive policies in place, such as no rentals. Generally company title apartments sell for less money than the equivalent strata title property but you have to remember that you may have difficulty selling it in the future because of the limited buyer pool.

Townhouses and villas are also strata titled and often appeal to down-sizers and/or young families who may not be able to afford a house yet want some outdoor space. Be mindful of supply and demand and scarcity, just as I've mentioned regarding apartments and house and land packages.

An important principle to be aware of is that the value is in the land, not the building. What I mean by that is that land goes up in value but buildings depreciate and ultimately need to be renovated or replaced. Land values will also vary depending on location. For instance, land close to the CBD is more expensive than land on the outskirts of the city. Scarcity is the main reason – there is simply not much land in smaller, developed inner-city suburbs while there is a seemingly endless supply of new land available for release in the outer perimeter. Then you have commute times to think of – people with higher incomes will pay for the privilege of shorter travel times.

As a final word on this, I encourage owner-occupiers to think like investors and investors to think like owner-occupiers when buying. For most of us, our home is our single greatest asset. If we choose well, not only will we have an enjoyable lifestyle, but when it comes time to upgrade or downsize, we'll have greater options than if we chose poorly. Investors need to consider who will live in the property, not only who their tenants might be, but who the ultimate buyer will be. Investors who choose property that owner-occupiers would like to buy in the future will experience greater capital growth than those who buy poor quality 'investor stock.'

CHAPTER 3

THE GROUNDWORK: MASTER THE MONEY SIDE OF PROPERTY

THE DEPOSIT

The biggest hurdle first-home buyers have to overcome is saving your deposit, especially if you're buying in a capital city.

It's ideal to aim for a 20 percent deposit, although many lenders will let you borrow up to 90 percent of the purchase price.

If you already own a property, you might have enough equity in it, which will mean you can tap into that for your deposit. This is one of the beautiful things that happens when you buy a property that goes up in value – you can use that increased value instead of having to save for another deposit!

Now, having the deposit is only part of the story, as there are a few more significant expenses that you will need to budget for.

LENDERS MORTGAGE INSURANCE (LMI)

If you are borrowing more than 80 percent of the value, you'll need to factor in LMI as an additional cost. This is an insurance policy that covers the bank in the event that you can't make your mortgage repayments at some stage in the future.

The cost varies from bank to bank so, to be safe, allow 2 percent of the amount you will be borrowing. Obviously you want to avoid paying this additional cost if possible. However, sometimes it simply won't suit you to wait until you can save more money, such as when prices are rising faster than you can save. In these cases, paying LMI does give you the opportunity to get into the market earlier.

If you are a professional such as a doctor, lawyer or accountant, however, you can probably get a deal where you won't need to pay LMI. The banks see people in these professions as being 'less risky' so they're often happier to lend them more money.

As of January 2020, eligible low and middle income first home buyers will have the opportunity of a government guarantee if their deposit is less than 20%. Qualifying buyers will be able to avoid paying LMI. There's further information available on the First Home Loan Deposit Scheme (FHLDS) via this link: www.nhfic.gov.au.

HOW TO PAY THE DEPOSIT

Weirdly enough, in this digital age, the easiest way to pay a deposit for a property (and you'll normally need to hand over 10 percent when you sign the contract) is by personal cheque. I say this because you can carry the cheque book in your pocket and write out a cheque when needed as opposed to getting a special clearance to transfer large amounts of money from your bank account. So ask your bank if they'll give you a cheque book or a handful of counter cheques.

If you don't have a cheque book you could get a bank cheque drawn before the auction. If the auction is held on a weekend, make sure you do this on a Friday. There are two issues with bank cheques, however, which is why I prefer personal cheques. Firstly, you need to get the cheque for an amount that is 10% of your maximum bid. If it turns out you can buy it for a lot less, this could be a little embarrassing for the agent after the auction! One way around this is to ask for a fixed deposit amount to be agreed prior to the auction. If, for example, your limit is going to be $950,000, you could ask for an amount that is more than 5% but less than 10%, say $70,000. That way, if agreed, your deposit amount will be $70,000 regardless of the purchase price. The second issue is that when you get a bank cheque you are withdrawing the money from your account, so if you aren't successful at auction, you won't earn any interest on that money until you return the cheque to the bank.

You can also transfer the funds electronically into the sales agent's trust account. Real estate agents usually hold the deposit money in trust for their owners from when the deposit is paid until the property settles and the new owner gets the keys. Trying to arrange the transfer of a large amount of money can get messy on auction day, though, and not all agents like this method (because often buyers don't realise they can only transfer $5,000 a day unless they've made prior arrangement with their bank). You'll have to make sure well in advance that your daily limit will allow a large transaction.

There is a new solution that has recently been launched by Macquarie Bank and has been adopted by some agents. It's called *DEFT Auction Pay*. As long as you have enough funds in a bank account that allows direct debit withdrawals, all you need to provide if you are the successful bidder at auction is your BSB, account number and a valid email address. It's a bit like BPAY for auctions. This is an easy solution if the agent offers the option.

My least preferable method is via deposit bond. A deposit bond is basically a bank guarantee that you can come up with the money. It's expensive and clunky and usually means your funds are tied up and not earning any interest while you hunt for a property. Some solicitors won't agree to their use. It's a last resort.

The safest place for your money while you're looking is the bank, using term deposits while you are saving. There's a good episode of my podcast that elaborates on this, and you'll find it at www.getauctionready.com.au/bonus.

STAMP DUTY

The biggest additional cost is stamp duty, which is a transaction tax applied by the state or territory government. The amount varies from state to state but you need to allow somewhere between 3 and 5.5 percent of the purchase price. Ouch!

Check your local Office of State Revenue website, they'll be sure to have a calculator.

Examples of stamp duty payable:

	$500K	$700K	$1M	$1.5M
NSW	$17,932	$26,932	$40,432	$67,802
Vic	$21,970	$37,070	$55,000	$82,500
Qld	$8,750	$17,350	$30,850	$59,600
WA	$17,765	$27,265	$42,615.50	$68,365.50
SA	$21,330	$38,245.50	$57,340.50	$89,165.50
Tas	$18,247.50	$26,747.50	$40,185	$62,685
ACT	$11,400	$20,040	$36,950	$68,100
NT	$23,928.60	$34,650	$49,500	$74,250

Note: these are estimates only, using each Office of State Revenue calculator, based on a property purchased after 1 July 2019. First-home buyers are eligible for concessions in most jurisdictions.

BANK FEES

The bank may have some charges to add to the tally. These include loan establishment fees, document fees and bank valuations, which could set you back another $1,000–$1,200 with some banks.

DUE DILIGENCE COSTS: LEGAL FEES & BUILDING/ PEST INSPECTIONS

Then there are the due diligence costs. It's safe to factor in $2,000–$3,000 for legal fees, including all the additional costs for disbursements (charges for various certificates and documents that your conveyancer or lawyer will need to order on your behalf) and reports.

If you are buying an apartment or townhouse, you will need to order a strata report, which is an account of the strata records and covers meeting minutes, financials, sinking-fund or capital-works-fund forecast, details of defects and repairs, squabbles between owners … This will cost upwards of $250 and you may also need a second report for the community property if it's in a large complex with community facilities. Please note that there are no set standards for strata reports and they aren't easy to interpret, so check out my video that outlines what to look for on www.getauctionready.com.au/bonus before you read one.

If you are buying a house, you should get a building and pest inspection, which will set you back around $600–$800. In some circumstances you will need both!

$500K purchase price	10% deposit	20% deposit
Deposit	$50,000	$100,000
Stamp duty (roughly)	$18,000	$18,000
Due diligence (up to)	$4,000	$4,000
Bank charges (roughly)	$1,000	$1,000

$500K purchase price	10% deposit	20% deposit
Rates at settlement (approx.)	$500	$500
Lenders mortgage insurance (example)	$9,000	Nil
Total you need to save	**$82,500**	**$123,000**

See the chapter on due diligence later in the book for more information.

COUNCIL AND WATER RATES

When it comes to settlement day you will need to repay the vendor for your portion of any council and water rates that have been paid in advance. Allow around $500 (but remember that this amount will vary from property to property and will depend on the point in the quarter that you settle) and remember that you will be liable for all of the rates from the next quarter forward!

BUYER'S AGENTS

If you want a shortcut to getting auction ready, put this book down and engage an exclusive buyer's agent.

An experienced buyer's agent can help you if you've found a property that you'd like to buy and you want to get expert advice on whether it's a good property or not, have all of the due diligence done for you, get expert pricing analysis and a recommendation of what you should pay, and then negotiate or bid for you at auction.

You can also choose to engage a buyer's agent to undertake your entire property search. This is great for people who are time poor, don't live near where they want to buy or are simply not interested in the property hunt.

Service	Percentage fee	Fixed fee	Limitations
Full property search	Different agents charge fees ranging from 1% to 2.5% of the purchase price.	Scaled according to price bracket OR determined by individual search parameters. Examples range from $8,000 to $50,000+.	Some agents put time limits & geographical limits – others will work until you have bought a property. Most require payment of a retainer and some charge progress fees.
Single property evaluation & negotiation	Percentage of purchase price (lower rate than the full search percentage).	Examples range from $2,000 to $10,000, dependent on the property type.	This service is specific to one property that you have found through your own searching.
Auction bidding	Percentage of the purchase price is more uncommon.	Most often a fixed fee – some include a success component.	Success is largely determined by your budget and the agent cannot advise you on suitability of property nor bidding limit.

A really good buyer's agent can help you even if you have heaps of time, live locally and love looking at property. They'll give you insights into the property market and how it operates. They'll protect you from getting carried away when you fall in love with a property. They'll handle the agents and level the playing field. After all, you've got to remember that you buy a property once every decade or so while the really active agents might be selling one or more per week.

Fees vary quite significantly and you can find out more at www.getauctionready.com.au/bonus.

That said, I'm assuming that you want to do this yourself, so keep reading ...

FINANCE APPROVAL

Once you have enough money to cover the deposit and all the purchasing costs you'll need to get your finance approved. I recommend talking to a few mortgage brokers while you are still saving and choosing one you feel comfortable with. A good rule of thumb is to find one with at least five years' experience, who asks you insightful questions (not just about now, but where you want to be in the future) and doesn't look at you blankly when you ask them to advise you on a borrowing strategy.

? WHAT IS A BORROWING STRATEGY?

An experienced broker will take into account your current circumstances as well as look to the future and consider your risk profile. They will then recommend a lending institution and type of loan that best suits you.

Different banks offer different loan features, such as offset accounts or the ability to pause repayments while on maternity leave. Some banks are more flexible than others. Quite often those who offer the lowest interest rates are the least flexible, which can end up costing you in other ways over the longer term.

A borrowing strategy will also take into account the pros and cons of paying lenders mortgage insurance and whether you should fix interest rates or keep all or part of the loan on a variable rate. It may also factor in a period of time when you make interest-only repayments.

If you have more than one property, your borrowing strategy must include deciding whether to cross-collateralise the loans (when one property is used as security over another) or keep them completely separate.

EIGHT QUESTIONS YOUR MORTGAGE BROKER SHOULD ASK YOU:

1. How long are you planning on owning this property?

2. Do you see your family situation changing (for example, kids)?

3. Is it likely you will quickly outgrow the property?

4. Will you ever consider renting it out?

5. Do you consider yourself to be a 'saver' or a 'spender'?

6. How are you planning on paying the deposit?

7. Have you factored in the cost of maintenance, repairs, renovations?

8. Do you have a buffer and, if so, for how long?

Your broker will advise you on what you'll need to do in the lead up to applying for your loan and which documents you'll need to provide. They will also let you know how much you can spend and what needs to happen before you will get unconditional approval. This is really important because it means the bank *will* lend you the money for the specific property you are looking at buying.

DOCUMENTS FOR BANK APPROVAL

To get a bank loan approved you need to prove a few things with additional documentation

Prove WHO YOU ARE
- Valid driver's licence
- Valid passport
  - If not both, Medicare/birth certificate
  - NB: marriage certificate if ID not updated yet
- Non-citizens
  - Up-to-date visa

Prove WHAT YOU EARN
- Last two payslips (must be last two) and bank statement that matches the payslip amounts, showing you are paid that amount
- If a bonus is to be counted, last two years PAYG and letter confirming your bonus/payslip
- Self employed/director of any companies on ASIC register
  - Last two years tax returns, NOAS and accounts
    - Personal
    - Business
    - Trusts
- Property owners - last rental statements

Prove WHAT YOU OWN
- Latest rates notice for all property
- Last three months savings statement with your name on it and the balance
- If over 50, super statements
- Shares - register summary with your name to match

Prove WHAT YOU OWE
- Last six months for any home loans with a statement with your name on it to match
- Last three months credit cards/car loans/leases
- HECS summary

Prove WHAT YOU SPEND
- Some banks may require a bank statement of your expenditure for three months plus any credit cards
  - If not, a detailed summary of your costs in a number of categories
- How much your rent you pay

Personal details
- Any credit issues - be upfront and tell lender prior to submission
- Dependants' ages
- Mother's maiden name
- Nearest relative name/address/phone
- Address history - three years
- Work history - three years and contact details

Source: Chris Bates

The first step, however, will be a pre-approval or an approval-in-principle and it's important to realise that this is not a guarantee that the bank will lend you the maximum amount for just any property. So it's my advice to keep in close contact with your broker throughout your search and let them know as soon as you find a property you are interested in. They'll then let you know if there will be any problems getting approval for that property and you need to consider alternative lenders or whether this should be a deal-breaker.

There is a lot involved in getting your loan structured so it best suits you now and in the future. By understanding the way mortgages work and how savvy property owners are able to get significant interest rate discounts, you can save a lot of money over the life of your loan. My podcast co-host Chris Bates is a mortgage broker and he's written a bonus chapter that explains what you need to know. You can download this for free on www.getauctionready.com.au/bonus.

FORMING YOUR A-TEAM OF PROPERTY EXPERTS AND SPECIALISTS

There's a lot of due diligence to be done before you buy a property and I'll cover that later in the book. Some of this can be done by you but you'll also need to know where to source other advice. It's prudent to know exactly who to turn to before you need them.

I've already spoken about the importance of establishing a relationship with an experienced **mortgage broker.**

I recommend also talking to an **accountant** who specialises in tax planning. This is particularly important for investors, who will be looking for ways to minimise their tax. Whether you're buying your first home, 'forever' home or an investment property, an accountant can advise you on ownership structure, finance structure, asset protection and how to minimise your tax burden both now and in the future.

The next person to line up is a **property lawyer** or **conveyancer.** Please don't think that any old lawyer will do. It's important to understand that a property specialist can help you avoid pitfalls that a generalist won't even realise exist. Find out their fee structure and ask how many contract reviews are included in the price. Some will charge you a fixed fee and include a number of reviews; others will charge you a smaller amount for every review and then the full fee when you buy. Paying a little extra to have a contract checked BEFORE you make an offer or bid at auction is a very wise investment. At the time of writing, I recommend you allocate around $2,000–$3,000 for legals.

If you're buying a house, you'll need a **building and pest inspector** on short dial. A licensed building inspector will check the structure and give you a report that will outline any problems, their magnitude and how this property compares to others of a similar age. A licensed pest inspector will check for termites and other pests that you don't want to be sharing your home with. My preference is to get an inspector who is licensed to do both jobs. Ask around your friends and family for a recommendation, not the local real estate agent, because, let's face it, they'll want a favourable report and you want an honest one! Your lawyer or conveyancer may also have one they use. Make sure they are prepared to meet you at the property at the end of the inspection so they can walk you through their observations and recommendations. There's more on how to get the best out of them in the chapter on due diligence.

If you're buying a strata property (unit, apartment, villa or townhouse), you'll need to get a **strata report** (it might have a slightly different name, depending on which state you're in). Speak to your lawyer or conveyancer first, as they may have a recommended supplier. Otherwise, you can google 'strata report' followed by your state. All reports are not equal and the cheapest will not be the best. Ask for a copy of a sample report. A good one will have a lot of detail, right down to copying email correspondence between the manager and committee members. I'll go into this in more detail in the due diligence chapter.

It might also be advisable to engage a **financial planner**, particularly if you are buying an investment property. A financial planner is a qualified investment professional who will help you achieve your long-term financial goals. They will advise you on insurance, superannuation, borrowing strategy, investments, saving, budgeting, etc.

Never engage a planner unless they are independent, charge a fee for service (i.e. no commissions) and understand property. The problem with engaging a planner who doesn't fit these criteria is that their advice can be biased if they are paid a commission on the funds they manage on your behalf. Since your home is probably going to be the most expensive thing you'll ever buy, if they aren't property-savvy you could be making poor decisions without the benefit of expert guidance. Unfortunately that narrows down the field considerably but it's worth seeking one out. They'll ensure that you buy now with the future in mind and they'll also advise you on the appropriate insurances to put in place to protect you and your assets.

MANAGING YOUR EXPECTATIONS AHEAD OF COMMENCING YOUR PROPERTY SEARCH

THE C-WORD

Compromise. There, I've said it. Nobody really likes to do it but unless you have limitless funds, you'll need to address it at some stage. My advice is to consider your 'must-haves' and 'would-likes' before you start. This is even more important if you are not the only decision-maker. More on that in a moment.

YOUR WISHLIST

Write a list of everything you want in a property: the suburb, the architectural style, the number of bedrooms, bathrooms, living rooms, outdoor space, parking, what's nearby, access to work ... Think about your needs now and in five years, and then in 10 years. It costs a lot of money to buy and sell property, so it pays to anticipate your medium-term requirements. Your needs will determine what you are looking for: a first home, a 'forever' home or an investment property.

Then divide the list into two: the things you CANNOT live without and those you can be flexible on. At this point I recommend jumping online and looking at the 'sold' section of the real estate portals. Check out recent sales in the areas in which you'd like to buy and be really honest about what you can get for your money. This is when you'll need to start considering whether to compromise on either the property or the location. Believe me, every search hits this fork in the road at some point, so best to tackle it at the very beginning.

COMPROMISING WITH YOUR PARTNER

When buying a home with a partner the challenge of deciding what to compromise on is magnified! It's important for couples to be firmly on the same page, but this process can take some time. Even when both partners seem to agree, there are often subtle differences in what each wants, which can make it hard to come to a point of decision. Often these differences don't even show up until one of you finds a property you really like.

Some couples start the buying journey thinking that they are completely aligned. I like to test whether this is really the case, by getting them to complete two separate wishlists, because any differences have to be identified and acknowledged before compromises can be agreed upon. Couples who are scared to disagree often float around making no commitments. On the other hand, couples who never agree tend to focus on their differences and ignore what is often a great deal of common ground! Once the deal-breakers for each partner are on the table and discussed at length, they can start to work out which compromises they can both live with. This is why it is important for both partners to be actively involved in the property search.

I suggest that you each write your wishlists separately then meet and compare notes. Then compile a joint list starting with the things you both want. These will become the must-haves. Then list the things you differ on. These need to be discussed and negotiated. But don't try to come to agreement at this stage, because this conversation is sure to continue throughout your property search and will develop with each and every property you consider.

Go and inspect properties together. Don't let one half do all the work unless they are the sole decision-maker. Once you have both inspected a number of properties and got a handle on what your money will buy you in your chosen area/s, revisit your list of differences. Often at this stage you will have a more realistic idea of what you can afford and may have even adjusted your own thoughts on what you are prepared to compromise on.

The quicker you recognise the differences and work out acceptable compromises the sooner you will buy your home and get on with life.

CASE STUDY

Julie and Richard had been looking for a larger family home for two years without success. The big problem, it seemed, was that Richard would never pay market value. Julie would do all the legwork, inspecting properties mid-week and presenting the shortlists to Richard. Every now and then she'd convince him to inspect a place that she felt would suit them and would be within budget. Without fail he'd scoff, invariably saying, 'That's overpriced, I could never justify paying what they're quoting.' He told her he wanted to upgrade but he never behaved like he wanted to.

The trouble was that Julie was a stay-at-home mum and every day she felt that they were outgrowing their home. Richard, on the other hand, spent five days a week at the office and worried about getting a larger mortgage.

Demoralised, Julie (pretty much literally) dragged Richard into my office.

We discovered that Richard felt that if he was to take on more debt, he wanted to feel like he got a lot more for his money. He wanted a larger block of land, which meant moving away from where they had been living for the past nine years. Of course, Julie wanted to stay close to her community and within walking distance of cafes and shops.

We then asked them about what else was important in a home and in a location. What did they spend their weekends doing? Where did their friends and family live? We also discussed the changes ahead once their kids started school.

Armed with all of this knowledge we researched suburbs where they could find other people like them, experience the lifestyle they wanted and, importantly, where the type of property they required was within budget. By opening up the conversation they were able to open their eyes to other possibilities. They spent the next few weekends checking out different suburbs rather than Julie dragging a reluctant Richard through houses he'd never agree to buy. When they decided on an area they'd be happy to live in, the property search started in earnest, with both of them on the same page. They bought within two months and they're all very happy!

DO YOUR RESEARCH TO FIND A PROPERTY

OPEN-HOUSE INSPECTIONS

I expect by now that you've been out inspecting properties. If not, you need to start! This process will help you to understand what you like, what you'll get for your money, and what property in your desired area is really worth. You'll also start to learn about how to deal with agents.

Begin by looking in your ideal suburb and be honest with yourself about whether you can afford to buy the sort of property you want. If you can't, make a decision quickly about whether you will change location or compromise on the property.

ATTEND AUCTIONS

I'm amazed at the amount of times I hear a buyer say that the first auction they ever attended was the one where they bought their home. Attending multiple auctions is really fundamental for anybody preparing to bid.

On-site or in-rooms

Most property auctions are held either 'in-rooms' or 'on-site.' On-site are usually held on a Saturday at the property. In-rooms are usually held on a mid-week evening in the real estate agent's offices or a hired space.

It's easier to see how many likely competitors there will be at an on-site auction, as opposed to in-rooms auctions, since there is only one property auctioned at a time. In most states, you'll need to register to bid so you can get there early and see for yourself how many bidders are registered. In Victoria, Western Australia and Tasmania, bidders don't need to register, so you'll just have to watch body language and guess.

> ## ❗ BODY LANGUAGE TIPS
>
> There is no uniform auction-bidder body language because people respond to stress in different ways. Look for signs of agitation (you might well be showing the same signs!) or notice who else is trying to size up the potential competition (like you are right now!). Some would-be bidders are so eager they arrive at the pre-auction open house before the agent, while others are trying to be cool and rock up at the last minute. Some bidders don't want to be distracted, so they'll be a lone ranger, while others bring a support crew of friends and family. One thing they won't be is calm.

With in-rooms auctions there are usually a number of properties being offered and it's difficult to tell how many people are interested in each individual property. Often the first two properties auctioned will be popular, with a couple of lacklustre ones in the middle and a competitive one at the end of the list.

Attend as many auctions as you can and you will see that no two are alike. Watch how different auctioneers work the crowds. See how some agents interact with buyers and others hang back. Watch bidder body language. Pay attention to what happens when the bidding doesn't reach reserve.

Different auctioneers

Not all auctioneers are equal. Some are highly accomplished. Some can barely count.

Some auctioneers only conduct auctions. That's all they do on a Saturday: race from auction to auction, battling traffic in-between.

Some sales agents are also auctioneers. This is more common in (though not limited to) outer suburban areas.

The difference between a selling agent acting as an auctioneer and an auctioneer who comes in on the day will be that the selling agent/ auctioneer will know the buyers best. Professional agents will have developed a relationship with buyers throughout the sales campaign and this creates a different style of auction. When the agent hires an auctioneer, they will brief them just prior to the commencement of the auction.

If the auctioneer comes and chats with you before the auction, he or she is probably trying to coach you. They'll encourage you to be the first bidder, possibly through overtly giving you reasons why it's a good thing to do, or more subtly by simply being warm and friendly. When the auction starts and they look you in the eye and ask you if you'd like to bid, you'll find it's harder to turn them down.

As a general rule, the boutique agencies and large individual franchise agencies engage a higher calibre auctioneer than a modest suburban real estate office can. At the upper end of the spectrum, auctioneers are highly trained and practised in reading body language, playing on emotions, controlling the crowd and, ultimately, getting people to bid.

At the other end of the spectrum, you'll see auctioneers who sound like they're calling a horse race, barely connect with the crowd and have little impact on the outcome. If buyers want to bid, they'll bid; if they don't, they'll pass it in with little fanfare.

Once you attend a few different auctions you'll see why it's so important to do your research because by knowing what to look for you'll be able to recognise opportunities to bid strategically. More on this in chapter 9.

DIFFERENT AGENT TYPES

In my experience real estate agents typically fall into one of two categories – 'deal focussed' and 'process oriented.'

The first type is deal focussed. These are agents who jump to action when they have a buyer on the hook. They won't let a deal pass them by. They are opportunistic and often charismatic. They thrive on a sale and know that the only way they get paid is to sell, sell, sell, and they never lose sight of this.

These agents are able to understand their vendor's motivation and are able to find out their bottom line. They are very focussed on managing their vendor's price expectations (otherwise known as conditioning) so that they can get a deal together in a timely fashion once they have identified a buyer.

The more skilled agents in this category will be very charming and persuasive and you will want to buy from them, even if the property they are handling isn't ideally suited to your needs.

The less skilled 'deal-focussed' agents will resort to playing games and being a bit liberal with the truth. You'll be less likely to trust these guys (and girls, of course) and will probably not want to buy from them unless they happen to be selling a property that really suits you.

The second type of real estate agent is process oriented and much less focussed on getting a deal across the line. They often lack the necessary negotiation skills and are nearly always inadequate when it comes to reading people and their buying signals. Often inexperienced (although some old-school agents can be like this too), they will be led by their vendors, who generally don't know how to negotiate either. The chances of them having their vendor's price expectations under control are a lot lower than a deal-focussed agent. They may not have the skills to close the gap between a buyer at a low price and a vendor at a high one.

Often these agents follow a very rigid step-by-step process and aren't able to roll with the punches. Step one, then step two, then step three and don't get the order wrong!

Generally those who are the worst negotiators will give you the least information. They don't know how to use information to get an outcome. So buyers get frustrated with them and sometimes even give up in disgust. Or they dig their heels in and nobody gets anywhere.

I'll cover in more detail how to handle agents later in this chapter.

PROPERTY RESEARCH

Not every property will generate a competitive auction and you'll start to learn signs to look for as you continue your research.

Which inspections are busy versus quiet? An auction campaign typically runs for three weeks of open houses, with the auction on the fourth week. The first open house is often busy with both neighbours and active buyers. The real indicators will be the second and third inspections. If they're busy, this could be a popular property. If they're not, the agent is probably struggling with the campaign.

These clues will come in handy when you start to consider whether to make a pre-auction offer. I'll cover that in detail in chapter 6.

Understanding which properties get a lot of buyer interest is important because you ultimately want to buy something that goes up in value, right? A home that is very attractive to local owner-occupiers has the potential to grow in value faster over time than a property that appeals to a limited buyer pool.

PRICE RESEARCH

An essential part of the research phase is developing an understanding of property prices and market conditions.

Keep a note of the agent's price guide for each property you inspect then record the ultimate sale price. Also note whether it sold before, at or after auction. If it passed in, track how long it took to sell after the auction and how many adjustments were made to the asking price. I recommend keeping all the information in a spreadsheet. Believe me, it will come in handy later. You can download a template at www.getauctionready.com.au/bonus.

If a lot of properties are passing in and taking a long time to sell, buyers are in a strong position. If auctions are competitive and property is selling quickly for what looks like high prices, then the sellers are in the strongest position. This is useful intel for when it comes your turn to negotiate or bid. See chapter 5 for more information on buyers' and sellers' markets.

WHAT DO AGENTS KNOW THAT YOU DON'T?

I once heard it said that negotiating with a real estate agent is like trying to play poker with a blindfold on and one hand tied behind your back. It's true that you are outgunned – not just because they do this for a living, but because they do hold more cards than you do.

They know the vendor's situation

How many times do you hear buyers ask, 'Why are they selling?' It's a pointless question because the agent doesn't have to tell you and even if they do tell you the real reason, how will you know it's true?

The vendor will have given the agent a reason why they are selling. Sometimes this is the truth, other times the vendor isn't being

100 percent honest with their agent. They may have already bought elsewhere and not want their agent to know that they have to sell. They may be getting divorced and don't want this to influence the negotiations.

Skilled agents know exactly why the property has been put on the market and exactly the price they need to get in order to make a sale.

Not all agents are skilled to the same degree, of course, yet the fact remains that they still know more about the vendor's degree of motivation and price expectations than you do.

They know how many other buyers are serious

The agent is the one handing out contracts, booking building and pest inspections, arranging private viewing appointments, talking to other buyers and tracking contract changes with the solicitors. The agent knows exactly who is seriously interested. They know if those people have been under bidders or made offers on other properties within their agency. They know if they have a property to sell. They know a lot and you know nothing about these other buyers.

The agent also knows when there is little buyer interest. They know when you are the only one interested. And you won't. Unless you read on and learn to pick up on the clues.

They know the reserve price

Usually the reserve price won't be set until the day of the auction because the agent will want the vendor to take into account all of the feedback they've received from buyers throughout the campaign. There will be a written reserve. There will often be an unwritten reserve too. This is the price that they'll sell for if they have to. The agent may show you the written reserve during the auction if they want you to increase your bid. But you'll probably never really know the unwritten reserve.

They know how auctions work

Agents know exactly what to expect at auction. It's their world, their habitat and they speak the language. They know how to respond when unusual things happen, as they often do with auctions. They know how to get that property sold. This is why it's so important to do your research and attend as many auctions as possible before you actually bid.

HOW MUCH SHOULD YOU TELL THE AGENT?

No matter what, if you are interested in a property, you *have* to let the agent know. If you don't, they might sell it to someone else without you being aware.

The best way to show interest without giving anything away is to ask for a copy of the contract. It's rare for an agent to sell a property without letting all contract holders know beforehand.

Of course, the agent will be trying to get information out of you. Usually they will want to know three things:

1. Are you financed and ready to buy?

2. How much do you think the property is worth?

3. Do you have a property to sell?

Other than the first question, you don't need to give them answers. But often buyers feel like they should and get themselves in a sticky situation. So here's how to handle these questions.

Are you financed and ready to buy?

Tell them if you have finance approval! But don't tell them for how much. When an agent knows that you have your finance in place they'll take you and your offer more seriously.

How much you think the property is worth?

The best way to tackle this question when you are not ready to make an offer is to answer with another question. Try these:

- I'm still thinking that through, which recent sales do you think are the most comparable?

- I'll have to give that some thought, is there a price that the owner has told you they'll sell for?

The goal here is to get more information out of the agent instead of letting them get more out of you. Many times buyers are caught off guard with this question and give a figure higher than they would have if they'd had time to really think about it.

Of course, agents have loads of less direct ways to get you to reveal a dollar figure. They may tell you that another buyer is about to submit an offer around $X and ask if you'd be interested at that price. They might suggest that 'buyer feedback is around $X and nobody is talking $Y' just to gauge your reaction to the higher amount.

A good question to fire back at an agent using these types of tactics is:

- If someone does offer that price, is the vendor definitely going to sell?

With any direct or indirect questions about what you'd be prepared to pay, stick to replying with another question unless you are ready to make an offer. We'll cover everything you need to do to be ready to make an offer in chapter 6. You certainly don't want to be giving too much away around your price intentions before bidding at auction.

Do you have a property to sell?

Any agent worth their salt will want to know where their next listing is coming from and they'll hope it's from you. They'll want to come and do a market appraisal on your home and suddenly you are dealing with them as both a buyer and a prospective vendor. You don't really want to muddy the waters when you are focussed on buying a particular property.

Ideally you will have already done your research and chosen your selling agent before you start looking to buy. But if you haven't and you like the agent, buy yourself some time. Let them know that you'll start the process of selling only after you've bought. If, however, you know that you will have to sell quickly, my recommendation is to put your property search on hold until you have decided on your real estate agent.

Any agent who suggests they'll give you favourable treatment as a buyer if you list your property with them should be approached with caution. Never under any circumstances sign an agreement with them because they've just demonstrated that their vendor is not their highest priority.

WHAT QUESTIONS SHOULD YOU ASK THE AGENT?

As a general rule of thumb, only ask the agent questions when you need to know something. Don't ask questions because you think you should be asking questions and don't waste your breath asking questions when you won't be able to trust the answers. When you ask a question, make it specific, not vague.

Good questions to ask

The questions that are important for buyers to ask are those that will give you an understanding of the real estate agent's process. Specific questions around access for inspections and how they will communicate with you throughout the campaign are useful. Questions you should ask about the specific contract terms are covered in the due diligence section.

Asking why the owner is selling is a fruitless question. The market will dictate the price regardless of why the owner is selling. Of course, in a buyers' market, the owner's motivation for selling may help you negotiate harder. However, most agents won't divulge that anyway, so there is little to be gained by asking.

If, on the other hand, you've looked online and can see that this property has sold quite often over the past decade or so (more than once in a decade is a warning sign in most areas), ask the agent why it has changed hands so often. Sometimes properties do transact a lot because they are poor quality. It might have a serious damp problem or the neighbour is a nightmare, for example. Of course, the agent's not going to tell you that in so many words, but if there are no credible reasons for each sale, this might be a warning sign you should heed. Some types of property sell regularly because they are at entry level, a small unit for instance. It's important to understand why before you buy.

If you are looking at a strata property, ask how much the quarterly levies are. These should be advertised but they aren't always and they do vary quite a bit. If there are special levies, ask what they are for and how many more instalments are left to be paid.

Paying strata levies is a way to budget for the ongoing costs of owning a property. Strata levies cover such expenses as maintenance, saving for large scale upgrades and paying building insurance, all things that people who own houses ultimately have to pay for themselves.

Buildings with high levies often have a pool, gym, lifts and extensive gardens. You might be prepared to pay the higher levies if you'll use the facilities, otherwise they really are a waste of money.

Sometimes levies are high for a set period of time because they have to raise money for a particular purpose.

Don't just look at what the levies are now, read the strata report and see whether they've always been high. Then read all the meeting minutes and email correspondence to find out why.

Low levies aren't always a good thing. It could mean that the owners aren't on top of maintenance and have no money saved for big repairs.

If you are looking at an investment that is currently tenanted, ask how long the tenants have been there and speak to other local property managers about the current rent to find out whether it's at market rate or not. You can also ask for a copy of the tenant's ledger to see whether they pay on time.

If you want to make an offer, rather than just saying 'Will they take offers prior to auction?', ask something more specific like, 'I'm in a position to buy this prior to auction, what will happen if I make an offer?' And then listen to what they say because their answer will contain clues as to what your next step should be. I'll cover this in a lot more detail in chapter 6.

AN AGENT'S LIST OF DUMB QUESTIONS TO ASK

What are the water rates and council rates?
These are pretty standard for every property in a given suburb.

Why is the owner selling?
You probably won't get the real story, so why ask?

Will the owner take pre-auction offers?
Agents will usually give a glib answer to this vague question.

How many contracts are out?
You'll almost never get the exact number, what would you do with the information if they did tell you?

What's the rental estimate?
The sales agent will almost always give you an inflated figure.

WHAT ARE YOU COMMITTING TO?

When you buy a property at auction you are purchasing the property without a cooling off period. That means that when the hammer falls the highest bidder (as long as they've bid more than the reserve price) is legally committed to buying the property – there is no backing out, no opportunity to change your mind. You will need to have done all of your due diligence (more on that in chapter 5), have unconditional finance approval and have had your contract reviewed by a lawyer or conveyancer *before* you bid.

You will also need to hand over a deposit immediately after the auction. This is usually 10 percent of the purchase price, unless you've previously had a lesser figure agreed to. Refer back to chapter 3 for how the deposit should be paid.

After the pre-agreed period of time on the contract of sale (called the settlement period), you will be required to pay the balance of the purchase price and what's called 'complete the sale.'

The big thing to be aware of at this point is that once you buy at auction THERE IS NO TURNING BACK – so you'd better be very certain that it's the property you want!

CHAPTER 4

WHAT'S THE PROPERTY WORTH?

DEMYSTIFYING REAL ESTATE AGENT PRICE GUIDES

When you see a property advertised for auction you'll notice that they don't all have price guides. You then call or email the agent and you'll be given a quoted figure or range (unless you're in Queensland, where agents are not allowed to give price guides). These must be treated as a starting point only. Please do not rely on them and do not use them as a basis for determining what you will pay.

It's important to note that not all agents quote the same. Some habitually underquote while others make an honest attempt to be realistic. Remember also that they are human and sometimes they get it wrong so simply adding 10 percent to the guide price is not a good idea.

It's really important, as a buyer, you learn to interpret agent price guides and understand what an auction price guide is.

QUOTE IT LOW, WATCH IT GO. QUOTE IT HIGH, WATCH IT DIE.

Fundamentally, the agent price guide is a tool to get a reaction from buyers.

Agents have a saying: 'Quote it low, watch it go. Quote it high, watch it die.' If they quote it low, buyers will think they've got a chance. They'll take a contract, get a building and pest inspection, and organise all their other due diligence. Then they'll turn up at auction, they'll bid, and a whole bunch of bidders will be disappointed because only one person can buy the property.

If they quote it just right, and that means what it's worth, then lots of buyers will feel like they haven't got a chance of getting it. The likelihood is that they're not going to compete and it might sell just for what it's worth.

Sometimes, agents accidentally quote it a bit high, and I mean accidentally because nobody is going to deliberately quote a price that is higher than what they really expect.

WHERE DOES THE PRICE GUIDE COME FROM?

Before an agent lists a property, they usually conduct an appraisal and pitch their proposal against other selling agents. There is an obvious temptation to put a high estimated sales price if they think that will increase their chances of winning the listing. Many otherwise level-headed property owners can get blinded by a little price flattery. So in order to make these estimates more realistic, the agents are required by law to provide evidence of how they have arrived at their suggested sale price. What usually happens is that they end up providing a range. What they really believe is at the lower end and what they think the vendor wants is at the upper end. This is the range that is written on the agency agreement and they are not allowed by law to quote a lesser figure.

However, the vendor probably won't sell at the lower end of that range without some heavy persuasion and they'd need to be convinced that nobody would be prepared to pay any more. Thus begins the conditioning process, whereby the agent seeks to close the gap between what they think the property is worth and what the vendor wants for it.

Now sometimes the vendor is right and buyers are prepared to pay more than the agent thinks. During an auction campaign, it is not uncommon to receive pre-auction offers. When the vendor rejects an offer, the agent is usually required by law to adjust their quoted price to ensure it is not less than the offer that's been rejected.*

There are a few loopholes with this though, and if the agent has said, 'I'm not accepting that offer,' because it wasn't in writing, for instance, or it wasn't on a contract, or the vendor said that they're not accepting offers, then the agent can say, 'Well, look. I didn't actually receive any real offer' and they will ignore that rule.

The quoted price range is an essential component required to generate competition. If the agent is allowed to continue quoting a low starting price, they improve their chances of being able to build substantial interest and have a competitive auction. However, if they are forced to increase their quoting, their job is made all the more difficult.

HOW DIFFERENT MARKET CONDITIONS AFFECT PRICE GUIDES

A buyers' market is when conditions favour the buyer: prices are stagnant or falling, auction clearance rates are below 60 percent and supply usually exceeds demand. In a buyers' market, bidders will be cautious and reluctant to compete if they think somebody else

---

* Every state and territory has different legislation regarding underquoting. Suffice to say that the general principle is the same across all jurisdictions: agents are not to mislead buyers and must be able to justify how they have arrived at their price estimates.

is already prepared to pay top dollar or if the vendor has unrealistic price expectations. Even when there is good interest in a property, high vendor expectations can end up creating a sluggish auction.

A sellers' market is when conditions favour the seller: when prices are rising, auction clearance rates are over 70 percent and buyers worry that they will be left behind and priced out of the market. In a sellers' market, it seems that almost every property can generate buyer competition and agents don't have to be as acutely focussed on getting the quoted price guide exactly right.

> **!** The auction clearance rate refers to the percentage of properties that have been offered for sale by auction in a particular week that sold either prior to auction, at auction, or immediately after the auction. So it doesn't purely refer to properties that actually sold 'under the hammer'.

The bottom line here is to be aware of the quoted price and what impact that can have on the ultimate sale price. A low price guide can build substantial competition while a more realistic one can limit competition. So don't assume all agents are low-balling, there are some good buying opportunities with reasonably quoted properties.

WHAT'S AN AGENT'S LEGAL OBLIGATION?

Every state and territory in Australia has laws to prevent agent under-quoting. These laws are meant to make sure that the agent quotes a price that is realistic and close to the figure prospective buyers can expect the property to sell for.

IN NEW SOUTH WALES, AGENTS HAVE THREE OPTIONS FOR QUOTING AN AUCTION PRICE GUIDE:

1. Quote the exact price that they put on the agency agreement

This is the simplest to interpret. If the agent is quoting a price range, then this is what has been written on the agency agreement. Of course, in week two or three of an auction campaign this range could have been adjusted up or down, so at the very least it should reflect an up-to-date vendor price expectation. So for example, if they put $700,000-$750,000 on the agreement, that's what they'll quote.

2. Quote a single price

This figure would normally be the bottom of their price range. You can be fairly confident that if an agent is quoting $700,000, for instance, the range on the agency agreement will be $700,000-$770,000, as the allowable range is 10 percent above the lower price. That an agent will quote the bottom of the range is a fairly safe bet, but they can quote any price within their range, so be careful of making that assumption.

3. Not quote a price at all

This is probably the most infuriating option to deal with - the agent who refuses to quote a price and (if you are lucky) gives you a list of 'recent' sales, which is often neither relevant nor current. It might be that this agent is the one to buy from, because a lot of buyers will probably vote with their feet, so you might find they have fewer bidders at their auctions.

In NSW, the law says that this range can be no more than 10 percent above the base figure (the bottom figure in the range; $900,000–$990,000, for example) and no lower price can be quoted. Once an offer has been rejected by the vendor the agent can no longer quote less than that price.

In Victoria, agents must prepare a Statement of Information for prospective buyers, which contains the median price for the suburb, three comparable sales and a price estimate which is either a single figure or a range with maximum 10 percent variance.

In Queensland, as mentioned earlier, agents are not allowed to give a price guide. The best you'll get is a list of recent sales.

OWNERS WILL HAVE THEIR OWN PRICE EXPECTATIONS

I've mentioned earlier that an owner will have their own price expectation and, quite often, it's a bit more than you're prepared to pay. Now the agent needs to be careful about knowing about the owner's price expectation because if they know that the price they're after is way above market value, they don't want to be forced to quote a really high figure.

You've got to be aware that there's a game going on the whole time. The owner wants a particular price, the agent's trying to get it, but also knows that you won't want to pay that much. Somehow the agent has got to bridge that gap. In a sales transaction, the agent is working for the vendor, not for the buyer. The best protection you have as a buyer is to do your own research.

There is no point just adding a blanket 10 percent or $100,000 to every auction price guide. You need to do your homework in order to work out what the property is worth (or get a professional to help you) and then use that figure as a decision-making point for setting your limit to either go to auction or make an offer.

SOME AGENT TRICKS TO WATCH FOR

Regardless of which state or territory you are buying in, there will always be some rogue agents who will look for loopholes in the legislation. Here are some examples of how they might try to get around the rules when giving auction price guides.

Estimated selling price

Agents will give vendors an estimated sale price and they need to be able to justify how they came up with that figure. Underquoting laws are meant to prevent them going to the buyers and quoting less than they told the owner to expect.

> *The rogue's loophole: On the agency agreement a rogue agent will put the lowest range that they think they can get away with. They might even explain to their vendor why they need to do this and why the range on their agency agreement will be less than they really expect. Their promises to their vendor will be verbal of course.*

How to identify a rogue: Ask them why they are quoting their auction price guide. If they refer to recent sales that you know are inferior (because you've done your research, right?), you might be dealing with a rogue.

Tricky terminology

Many states have banned the use of phrases such as 'offers above' and 'offers over' as well as the use of symbols like a plus sign when publishing or stating the estimated selling price.

The rogue's loophole: This is all just semantics. Just because the words 'offers over' or 'above' can't be used doesn't mean that there is no 'invisible plus sign' after published auction price guides.

How to identify a rogue: Let's be frank, nearly every sales agent will publish the price at the bottom of their range as their auction price guide. They'd be mad not to. The intention remains as it always was – to be under where they think it will sell. Where the rogue differs is that they'll use some creative terminology in order to get around the rules. For example, they might say to buyers 'we've had serious buyer interest around $500,000' when they know damn well the vendor is expecting a lot more.

Agent record keeping of price statements

In some states agents are now required to keep a written record of any and all prices they have quoted in relation to each property they offer for sale by auction. This means that each and every time they tell a potential buyer their price guide, they need to document the conversation!

The rogue's loophole: This is an easy requirement to fulfil at open houses, but a nightmare for agents to record their phone conversations with prospective buyers. It's good time management to make calls while driving in their car between appointments, imagine having to pull over every five minutes to make a file note! The best way to get around this requirement is to simply avoid giving verbal auction price guides.

How to identify a rogue: Rogue agents are often very difficult to get hold of, hard to pin down and will often talk in riddles.

*Reference: Cath Dickinson,
'Underquoting quick guide', Real Estate Journal, January/February 2016 edition.*

Most professional agents are prepared to do what is required to comply with underquoting laws. They understand that buyers need quality information and transparency. They have to balance this need, of course, with their aim of creating competition so that an auction campaign delivers the best sale price for their vendor. It's a tricky path to navigate.

Property buyers need to remember that a selling agent is working for the vendor. It is my view that buyers need to do their own price research so that they can make up their own mind on what a property is worth. By knowing the signs of a rogue agent they can be better equipped to determine which price guides are pure fiction and avoid falling into the trap of wishful thinking. A buyer who recognises a rogue agent can also use this knowledge to their advantage and perhaps even force the price guide up to where it should be. This will give you a competitive edge.

For example, an agent is quoting $900,000 and you know that it's likely to be closer to $1.1M because you've recently seen similar properties sell in this range. You might be happy to pay $1,090,000. If you offered this amount and the vendor rejected your offer, then the agent is bound to change the quoting from $900,000 to $1,090,000. This would stop a lot of buyers who were hoping the property was going to sell for less than a million dollars and have a negative impact on the momentum they were hoping to build for the auction.

CASE STUDY

One thing to remember is that the vendor may still have a price in their mind that is much higher than what is written on the agency agreement. Savvy agents prefer them not to verbalise this (God forbid they should write it down!) and will be working hard to manage their expectations throughout the auction campaign. No underquoting laws will protect a buyer from dealing with an unrealistic vendor.

Having a vendor who refuses to let the agent put a low range on the agency agreement presents a conundrum for the sales person. The agent needs to generate buyer interest in order to have any chance at achieving a big price at auction and in order to build interest they need the lowest possible price guide. As a consequence, I've seen some creative real-estate auction underquoting.

Here's one example. A terrace in Paddington was advertised with a guide of $2.5M. After I made an enquiry about inspection times via the agent's website, I received a subsequent email volunteering that they had an offer of $2.3M. Yet there was no mention of whether the vendor had accepted or rejected the offer. It turned out that this was their way of lowering the quoting (without actually changing the price guide) when their vendor wouldn't allow them to reduce the amount on the agency agreement.

HOW TO ACCURATELY CALCULATE WHAT THE PROPERTY IS WORTH

The first thing I am going to say here is that there is one thing you must *never do*. Do not rely on those free automated valuation reports (AVM) you can get online. These are computer-generated reports that give a price estimate for a property. Most banks offer them, mortgage brokers will give you them and there are a number of free sites where you can get your own. Even the ones you pay for are not worth the paper they are written on (assuming you print it off, of course) because the algorithms they use are not equipped to deal with the variations and complexity of our property market without a large margin of error. It may change in the future as artificial intelligence gets smarter, but we're not there yet.

CASE STUDY

I recently downloaded 10 different automated valuation reports for a little terrace (two bedroom, one bathroom, no parking) in Tempe, which is the most affordable suburb in Sydney's Inner West, courtesy of its proximity to the airport.

This property went to auction in December 2018 and passed in, finally selling in January 2019.

The agent's price guide was $950,000 (which means they probably put $950,000–$1,045,000 on the agency agreement according to the Office of Fairtrading's guidelines)

The property passed in at auction and was subsequently listed with an asking price of $1,059,000.

AVMs often offer a very wide estimated price range. Here is one example:

Low	Mid	High
$892,500	$1,050,000	$1,207,500

They usually also recommend one price or a mid-point and there can be a vast difference from top to bottom:

1. *$985,000*

2. *$1,004,509*

3. *$1,030,000*

4. *$1,041,000*

5. *$1,050,000*

6. *$1,050,000*

7. *$1,074,000*

8. *$1,079,981*

9. *$1,099,711*

10. *$1,214,000*

That's a range of $229,000 on a property worth around a million dollars!

The ultimate sale price was $1,002,500.

Only one out of the 10 reports was on the money and just because they were close on this property does not guarantee that they would be the most reliable next time around. A staggering eight out of 10 of these AVMs recommended a price that was more than the property sold for.

Even if you downloaded all 10 reports, as I did, and worked out the midpoint of the estimates (which comes in at $1,099,500) you would have paid too much for this property.

Now I've convinced you that AVMs are useless at best, misleading at worst, you'll understand why you need to do your own research.

In my business as a buyer's agent we have an obligation to our clients and a requirement under the Property Stock and Business Agents Act 2002 (NSW) to undertake a thorough analysis when determining what purchase price we recommend a client pays. There's a lengthy list of factors we take into consideration in order to be confident with our recommendation.

COMPARABLE SALES

The most important thing to get a handle on is where the property you want to buy sits in relation to other properties in the area. The best way to do is to look at recent sales. These days the information is really easy to come across (and it's free!). Both domain.com.au and realestate.com.au have the facility for users to search for recent sales – just make sure you check the sale date as the more recent they are, the better. You can look at photos and floor plans, which are particularly helpful. Then you will be able to make comparisons based on location, size, accommodation, parking, architectural style and condition. Rank them from worst to best and then see where the property you want to buy fits in.

Other things that we take into account include:

- Assessment of the characteristics that may affect the price people are willing to pay for this property in the current market. What sorts of things do buyers in this area really value? Does this property possess them? For example, do buyers love Victorian terraces? If so, they'll give high value to period details and be less interested in properties that have had all the original features removed.

- Is it a property that will attract buyer interest if you need to sell it in a flat market? Is this always going to be popular with buyers? Or are there major compromises that most buyers won't like? For example, a property on a main road might sell quickly in a sellers' market because buyers will be more prepared to compromise when they fear missing out. That same property will struggle when the market slows down and buyers have more choice.

- Is there an obvious way that you can add value? A simple renovation, even a paint-job and some landscaping can result in an immediate increase in value. A good example is when a property has been tenanted for some time. The tenants won't be presenting the home as beautifully as an owner-occupier might and there's a good chance it needs new carpet, floors polished and a lick of paint. Improved presentation, as long as the property is structurally sound and has a good floorplan, can add immediate value.

IS THE MARKET GOING UP OR DOWN?

After you've worked out where this property sits in relation to the rest of the market you'll need to decide whether to adjust the price according to market conditions.

If the market is going up, prices will be rising and you'll need to factor that in so you don't get caught out always being the underbidder. In the next section I'll talk about how to set your maximum bid and in chapter 6 I'll cover when it's best to make a pre-auction offer. For the moment, cool your heels, don't make any offers until you've done all of your due diligence!

If the market is slowing down or falling, you'll need to ensure that you don't get caught out paying too much because you're looking at old sale prices.

In between the two is a transitional market, where buyers slow down but vendors take a while to catch on and still want their premium price. This can create inconsistencies with sale prices.

Here are some of the signs to look for:

- **Auction clearance rates**
  Every week you'll see these published in the Sunday papers. Or you can check out this link: www.domain.com.au/auction-results. As a basic rule of thumb in Sydney and Melbourne, clearance rates under 60 percent means a slowing or declining market, 60–70 percent mean a balanced or stable market and anything above 70 percent is a rising market. In Brisbane, where auctions aren't as prolific, a 50 percent clearance rate indicates the market is pretty strong.

- **Days on market**
  You can get suburb days-on-market data with this great free resource: www.residex.com.au/free-report. In a rising market the days on market won't matter because most properties will be selling in under four weeks. Days on market will matter in a balanced or slowing market as this figure will give you an indication of the severity of the downturn and the direction it's heading in. Days on market between 30 and 60 are not too alarming. However, when it takes longer than two months to sell the average property, it is clearly a buyers' market.

- **Vendor discounting**
  Vendor discounting is a percentage figure that shows how much owners have had to reduce their asking prices in order to get a sale. This is an important indicator in non-auction oriented areas, so it will be of little use to you here. I mention it only because in a true buyers' market, more property will pass in, which means they will be given an asking price and if this is too high, it will need to be discounted. Vendor discounting is an indicator of overall market conditions – it's also an indication of how realistic the original asking prices were.

A word of caution: the methodology used to arrive at these figures will vary from source to source, so it's important to make sure you use the same source of information every time you check.

HOW TO SET YOUR MAXIMUM BID

When you go to bid at auction, you need to set your top dollar (or maximum bid) beforehand, with a clear head. When you understand market value, along with any premium that you are prepared to pay if this home uniquely suits your needs, you are less likely to get drawn into a foolish competition. We ask our clients to consider the level at which they are prepared to let another buyer have it. It is crucial that you know this figure ahead of time and make a commitment to yourself to stick to it!

On the flipside, if you are the only bidder prepared to make a bid, or the highest bidder on a property that has passed in, by understanding the value you can confidently continue negotiations and know when a fair price has been reached, or when the vendor simply wants too much.

To start with, you need to forget all the other buyers and the vendor, just for a moment. This is about you and the property. It's about how uniquely this property suits your needs and how much you want to buy it.

FIVE KEY QUESTIONS TO ASK YOURSELF

You can't rely on the answer of any one of these five questions; you need to consider the whole lot:

1. **How much do you want it?**
   How long have you been looking for? Is this the only property that you have found in 12 months that you really like?

2. **How much does this property suit your needs?**
   What is your timeframe - own it for five years then upgrade, or is this your 20-year home? Are you an investor or an owner-occupier? Owner-occupiers might pay a premium as they will be living in the house but investors should be more hard-nosed and not let emotion be a factor. Is it really that unique? Or will there be others? For example, if you need three bedrooms and a study and most houses don't have the study, then when you find one with that extra room, you'll know it will uniquely suit your needs in a way most others in the area can't.

3. **How good is this property?**
   Not just in terms of how it suits your needs, but generally in the marketplace, how popular is it? Do other buyers want to own it?

4. **How much is this property worth compared to others in the area?**
   What is the current market value when you compare it to what has recently sold? This is where it's crucial that you have done your pricing research.

5. **How much can you actually afford?**
   Never make this decision without the guidance of a good mortgage broker.

As a general rule, if property is scarce and in demand, you'll need to consider paying a premium. The price research you have done if you followed the steps in the previous section will give you a firm foundation to work from.

Let's give you some examples:

If you only consider how much you want this property, or how much you can afford, you really do run a risk of paying far too much money for it. I've seen people set their auction bidding limit at their budget with no real regard as to what the property is actually worth.

CASE STUDY

Hugh had been looking for a home in his preferred suburb for about six months and was the underbidder at three auctions, only just missing out on each property by a few thousand dollars. He finally came to the conclusion that he needed to look elsewhere and fairly quickly found a suitable property in a less expensive suburb.

He felt confident that he would get this place because his budget of $900,000 was strong for this area. At the auction he got into a bidding war, which he won, partly because he was so sick of missing out and he just kept raising his paddle. He ended up paying $897,000.

Unfortunately though, this apartment wasn't worth the money. Hugh hadn't spent enough time looking in this new suburb to understand how different the values were. So he went to auction with his maximum budget as his bidding limit instead of the property's value. If he'd been patient, he would have been able to buy something else very similar for around $850,000.

On the other hand, if you only focus on what that property is worth in the context of the rest of the market, but it really, really suits your needs in a way that is unique, then you could miss out by not being prepared to pay a premium. Or, if you focus too much on what other buyers may or may not do, you run the risk of buying a property purely because you can, because you want to win, not because you really want it, or not because you really wanted to pay that price.

A helpful way to think about this is that if you bought it and woke up on the morning after the auction, at what price would you say, 'I am really happy with that', versus, 'I feel sick, I paid too much'? You really do not want buyer's remorse the next day.

Alternatively, if you woke up on the morning after the auction and you hadn't bought it, would you think, 'I really should have paid that'? Or, would you think, 'I'm relieved that other buyer paid way too much'?

By being really clear on what your maximum bid is going to be before you go to auction you are less likely to be unconsciously drawn into competition. Knowing the value of the property in question will enable you to confidently agree on a price, or know when it is wiser to let it go.

CASE STUDY

When I was a sales agent I never ceased to be amazed at the justifications buyers would give for either bidding or not bidding when they were feeling the pressure of the auction. Social proof is a big one – buyers who keep bidding because they think 'it must be worth it because that other person just bid.' If only they took a moment to wonder why they think the other person knows more about the property's value than they would.

On the flipside are buyers who stop bidding because 'that other buyer was never going to stop.' Many times, as a buyer's agent, I've bought a property on my very last bid because my bidding style gave no clue of my upper limit. More than once I've had the underbidder come up to me afterwards and say they had more money but they just gave up. If only they knew that one more bid would have bought the property ...

CHAPTER 5
DUE DILIGENCE

BUYER BEWARE: WHY YOU NEED TO DO DUE DILIGENCE AND TO HAVE UNDERSTOOD IT

Have you heard of the term 'caveat emptor'? It means 'buyer beware' and it applies when you buy property. When you sign a contract you need to be certain you know what you are doing, because you are buying that property as it is, in most cases with no warranty. The only time you get a warranty is within the first six years of some newly built or renovated properties where there exists a current home owners warranty certificate.

Over the years I've come across many buyers who have been unwilling to spend the money on pre-purchase inspections prior to an auction in case they miss out on the property. They see it as wasted money, particularly if they've missed out on a few auctions already. This is really insane. So many things can go wrong with property and repairs can be costly – vastly more expensive than a few hundred dollars for a report. I recently heard of a buyer who had to spend $25,000 replacing their roof within months of buying their home and another who had to completely replace a bathroom that had a leaking shower. And don't fall into the trap of thinking that other bidders must have ordered reports that have checked out – they could be doing the same as you.

Another thing buyers should never do is bid at auction without getting the contract reviewed by a lawyer or conveyancer. Some people are very cavalier about contracts and seem to think they are all the same. They are not! Auctioneers often tell war stories about buyers who bought without realising there were clauses in the contract that disadvantaged them. One story I recently heard was about a swimming pool that had to be removed because it didn't comply with council regulations. The buyer didn't get the contract checked before the auction and had no idea!

AVOID BUYING A LEMON: WHAT DUE DILIGENCE DO YOU NEED TO DO?

Information is power when it comes to buying property, so we must surround ourselves with experts in all the fields we need: finance, legal, building inspectors, architects, interior designers, property managers and trades people. Getting the right information from the appropriate professional can help you avoid buying a lemon. It can also assist you in knowing all the downsides of a property and this knowledge may be very useful when it comes to negotiating with an agent.

DUE DILIGENCE CHECKLIST

1. Contract of sale

2. Council checks

3. Infrastructure checks

4. Renovation potential - architect, builder

5. Unique issues - like pet approval in strata

6. Finance

7. Building and pest inspections

8. Other inspections - plumbing, electrical, etc.

9. Strata report

CONTRACT OF SALE

Have a lawyer or conveyancer on standby to review the contract of sale. Make sure you choose somebody who specialises in property, who can act fast and won't be tied up in court when you need them. There may be changes that they'll need to request, especially if you want to change the settlement date or pay less than a 10 percent deposit, so make sure you don't leave the contract review till the last minute. Never sign a contract without getting legal advice!

COUNCIL CHECKS

Most councils have a development section on their websites. Jump on there and look into whether any of the neighbours have lodged or are planning to lodge a development application.

Check out the zoning in surrounding streets. You don't want to find out that a whole bunch of eight-storey apartment buildings are about to be constructed around you.

If the property has a view, look at the planning controls to see whether there is a chance of that view being built-out.

When you've finished checking online, pick up the phone and call the council. Ask to speak to a duty planner and ask them anything you haven't been able to find out via their website. In particular, ask them if there are any changes on the horizon that will affect either this property or the surrounding ones.

INFRASTRUCTURE CHECKS

Look at the local and state government websites for infrastructure development that might impact on the property, in particular, roads and anything likely to create noise and devalue the property. In Sydney in recent years, WestConnex has been a major issue and property owners in a number of suburbs have been impacted by compulsory acquisitions, road widening, tunnelling and the location of new exhaust stacks.

You will probably need to do a bit of digging here. Once you uncover a likely project, such as a new road, airport, hospital, etc., check whether it's under construction, approved or simply planned. Then make Google your friend. Find out as much as you can, particularly if there are resident action groups. These will always focus on worst-case scenarios and not be subject to any sales spin.

RENOVATION POTENTIAL

If you are planning to renovate, do not make assumptions! The best way to verify whether your ideas are feasible is to engage a local architect to inspect the property and advise you. You want to be sure that the council is likely to allow you to make your planned improvements and also that the cost is expected to be within your budget. It may cost a few hundred dollars but that's a small price to pay to avoid buying something and then finding out you can't do what you wanted. All councils have an LEP – local environment plan – and a DCP – development control plan. The state government will also have an SEP – state environment plan. They set out guidelines for property improvements and new buildings. Then there are areas where complying development is OK, meaning you don't need to get council approval for building works as long as they meet a set of criteria.

UNIQUE ISSUES

Often buyers have unique needs that need to be accommodated in their home. If these are deal-breakers, do not assume you can sort them out after you buy. Get advice from specialists in the area.

If you have a pet and are buying an apartment or townhouse, approach the strata manager to find out whether your pet will be approved.

If you want to build a pool, make sure it's feasible and affordable. Get a pool specialist to advise.

If you need to install a lift, get a lift specialist to give you a quote and advise you of the planning requirements.

If you want to put a shed or workshop in the garden, check with council to make sure you keep within their size limits so you can avoid needing to get a development approval.

FINANCE

Make sure that your finance is approved and know whether you will need a valuation prior to going to auction. Ask your broker well in advance of the auction and make sure you understand whether there are any risks for you if you proceed without a valuation. The bank will not automatically lend you 80 percent of whatever price you pay for a property, they'll lend you 80 percent of what they deem the value to be. So if the valuation comes in at a figure that is less than what you pay, you'll need to make up the shortfall somehow.

BUILDING AND PEST INSPECTIONS

I would never bid for a property without having a building and pest inspection and most of the time we organise an inspection to be done by our regular licensed inspector. We meet the inspector at the end of the inspection to discuss any areas of concern.

We would only ever buy a building inspection report provided by the vendor or the agent under certain circumstances – like when we don't have time to organise our own report because someone else is about to buy the property and we have to move fast! Under those circumstances, after reading the report, we always call the inspector to get their verbal opinion on the property. It can often be markedly different to their written report. The reports have pages and pages of disclaimers and it's easy to get overwhelmed by them and not focus on the comments that are specific to the property in question. By speaking with the inspector you can get a sense of whether the overall condition is good, average or bad.

OTHER INSPECTIONS

Most building inspectors will recommend getting a separate plumbing and electrical report because these trades are outside their area of expertise and if repairs are needed, they can be costly.

They will certainly flag where they think expert advice is needed and we recommend getting to the bottom of any problems before you buy the property, not afterwards. For example, if the property has damp issues, the cost of repair will be determined by the cause. It could be a leaky pipe or it might be rising damp. Each of these will need different specialists to solve the problem and it's worth getting quotes so you know the extent of disruption and cost.

There have been plenty of times when we have had to get additional advice from specialist tradies. I can think of examples where we have had investigate asbestos removal, the health of a large tree, the condition of a retaining wall, and the cause of puddles under a house. Water is one of the chief causes of problems with buildings – it will always take the course of least resistance and wreaks havoc when it goes where it shouldn't! Leaks can go undetected for a long time before the damage starts revealing itself, by which time the remedy can be very expensive!

If there is a big tree in the backyard, get an arborist to check it and make sure it's healthy. They can also tell you whether it will grow any larger. You want to know whether the branches are in danger of falling or whether the roots are likely to cause problems with the stormwater, fences or building foundations.

Forewarned is forearmed. Sometimes, when a property is going to auction, other buyers do not do as thorough due diligence as we do. So they go to auction and pay more money than we would for the property and then get hit with a major repair bill within the first couple of years of ownership. At other times, when there is an obvious problem, other buyers can be scared off. If we can uncover the root cause of the problem and know the cost of fixing it, we can be very confident in our negotiations and really use the defects to get the price down.

FIVE QUESTIONS TO ASK YOUR BUILDING AND PEST INSPECTOR

1. **How does the building compare with others of a similar age?** You want it to be 'above average', but descriptors like 'typical' and 'average' are not deal-breakers in my opinion. Even 'below average' can be acceptable - as long as you can address the issues and pay a price that reflects the building's condition.

2. **Are there any active pests?** We still might buy a property if it had active pests - dependent on the damage done and how quickly they can be eradicated - as long as we can get a good discount on the price!

3. **Is there evidence of past pest activity that has caused damage and has not been rectified?**

4. **What immediate maintenance issues are there?** Sometimes it means getting a specialist in to give detailed advice (plumber, electrician, structural engineer, arborist, etc.).

5. **What ongoing maintenance issues should I be aware of?** The report should make mention of all issues, in particular where there is risk of future termite invasion.

If you are the only buyer who understands the full extent of the building issues, don't be afraid to walk away from the property if the vendor simply won't accept that there is a problem or if another, less informed buyer is prepared to pay more than you. When advising the agent of the issues, make sure you give them a copy of the relevant section of the inspection report. Back up your claims with hard evidence to show you are not playing games.

STRATA REPORT

When you're buying a strata property (apartment, townhouse, villa), you need to do an extra layer of due diligence. The first step is to order a strata report. Most people, when they get one of these, will glaze over and not know what to look for. There's important information contained in these reports and what's missing is also very telling. For example, we might notice in the minutes of the Annual General Meeting a mention of quotes obtained for drainage work yet no further reference anywhere else in the report. We would expect to see some email correspondence so we can understand why they got the quotes in the first place. I'd also like to see the quotes and to understand whether they were planning on proceeding with the work. When further details are missing it can simply mean that the strata manager is really bad at keeping records, or at its worst it can mean that the owners' corporation is consciously avoiding documenting a problem, which can be a major issue.

The first thing you need to understand is that the quality of reports is highly variable and can only be as good as the quality of the information that's made available for the inspector.

Not all strata managers are the same and some are terrible at keeping records ... There's no standard that you can rely on and random things can impact on the report quality – for instance, sometimes an important file is actually on the strata manager's desk at the time of inspection. If the building is self-managed, it can be very difficult to get up-to-date information.

Don't rely on your solicitor to review the strata report, as they aren't necessarily qualified in this area. You'll need to read and understand the report yourself.

A good report should have a list of documents that the inspector expected to see. Take a note of what's missing and start a list of questions you will ask either the strata manager or the agent.

LIST OF DOCUMENTS INSPECTED FOR A STRATA REPORT (NSW)

Strata Roll

Strata Plan

Certificate of Title

Financial Accounts

Capital Works Fund Forecast

Building Valuation for Insurance

Building Insurance Certificate

AGM (Annual General Meeting) Minutes for previous 5 years

ECM (Executive Commitee Meeting) Minutes (if they have meetings between AGMs)

Correspondence File

Fire Safety Certificate

Workplace Health and Safety Report

Asbestos Report

Source: Eyeon

SAMPLE QUESTIONS TO ASK THE STRATA MANAGER OR SALES AGENT

Why has the owners' corporation decided not to follow the recommendations for fund balances in the Capital Works Fund Forecast?

There isn't much money in the Capital Works Fund, so are they proposing a special levy to pay for remedial works that are noted in the AGM minutes?

We note that there is only one person on the executive committee - is there a problem with harmony in the building?

There are many mentions of water leaks in the AGM minutes but nothing in the correspondence file, surely there must be an email trail on the subject?

Many people only look at the financial accounts when they get a strata report but there is a lot more than money to be mindful of. Fundamentally you need to be confident that they are raising enough funds to run the building as well as putting enough away for larger capital works. It's not uncommon for buildings to incur large bills when the roof needs replacing, windows need to be upgraded, all the common areas painted or lift replaced, to name a few.

Look for the Capital Works Forecast – in NSW every building has to have one done, however, there is no requirement to get a good one, nor to follow the recommendations.

Firstly, check whether the Capital Works Forecast is current. Then look at how detailed it is (or is not). Was it done by a quantity surveyor and does it contain a table with a recommended fund balance for every year for the next twenty years? Some owners' corporations purchase the cheapest option, which is generic and contains little information that is specific to that building.

Look very carefully at the minutes from the Executive Committee Meetings to see whether there has been any discussion about upcoming special levies or building works that look like they will cost more than they have in the Capital Works Fund. Special levies are payments that owners have to make over and above the standard strata levies when there is not enough money in the kitty to pay for necessary building works.

Check whether GST is payable on the strata levies or whether their total income is close to the level where they'll need to register for GST (currently this is $75,000 pa for a 'profitable' enterprise and $150,000 pa for a 'non-profitable' one). If they do need to register for GST, this will mean an immediate 10 percent levy increase!

> **!** Say your levies are currently $1,000 a quarter and every year the total amount collected from owners for levies is $145,000. They only need a small increase in levies to take them over the $150,000 threshold to register for GST. When this happens, your quarterly levies will go up to $1,100 overnight.

Remember that buildings are run by people, which means that disputes are a very real possibility. There are clues to be found in the email correspondence between committee members and the strata manager – is there evidence of any disharmony?

Check the bylaws for anything that might impact on your lot – and be aware that the bylaws in the report may not be completely up to date (although there should be a full set in the contract of sale, so you can cross-reference). An example would be a bylaw that allowed your neighbour access to the roof above your apartment. You'd want to make sure they couldn't put a garden in without proper waterproofing.

History is the best predictor of the future, so any building less than twenty years old should be approached with caution as a large proportion have major defects to address and many find themselves in litigation.

You don't have to rely on a third party to provide you with a report – you can go in and inspect the records yourself. They will be kept at the strata manager's office and you'll need a letter of authorisation from the sales agent before you call to make an appointment.

Regardless of whether you order a report or inspect the records yourself, make sure that you ask questions whenever there is something missing or there's anything you don't understand. If the strata manager won't speak to you, talk to the person who provided the report (ideally both). If you can't get satisfactory answers, ask the selling agent to find out. They are required to find the answers for you.

A strata report is an essential part of the due diligence process and it's something to be read and understood. You really must do everything possible to avoid the potential cost and stress that will result from buying into a poorly run building.

CHAPTER 6

BEFORE AUCTION: BUYING BEFORE AUCTION DAY

KNOW YOUR NEGOTIATION OPTIONS

When you're interested in a property that is being marketed for sale by auction, you have to consider three options for making an offer or bidding.

1. PRE-AUCTION OFFER

This is where you try to buy the property before the auction. The offer will need to be enough to entice the vendor to sell without waiting for what they hope to be a competitive auction that will push their price up. You will also need to be ready to buy the property under auction conditions, which means no cooling off period. It's highly unlikely that an agent is going to kill the momentum of a good marketing campaign to give you the opportunity to change your mind and back out of the deal.

It's important to note that buying prior to auction isn't always an option. Sometimes the circumstances of the sale will prescribe that the property has to go to auction. It might be a deceased estate, or the owners could be getting a divorce, or there might be a court order that says it must go to auction. In a sellers' market, many agents will avoid taking pre-auction offers. It's not always the best option for a buyer either, as other buyers can enter the fray and you won't necessarily know how much they've offered.

Table showing cooling off periods before auctions by state

	Standard
NSW	You can waive the cooling off period by giving the vendor a 66W Certificate.
Vic	If your offer is accepted less than three clear business days before or after the auction date, you do not get a cooling off period.
Qld	You can waive the cooling off period prior to the auction without needing a solicitor by completing an REIQ form.
WA	No cooling off period on an offer made within the three days before or after an auction.
SA	The standard cooling off period is 2 days. If you buy a property at auction or on the day of the auction you are not entitled to a cooling off period.
Tas	There is no cooling off period for private treaty nor auction sales.
ACT	You can waive the cooling off period by getting a signed certificate from your solicitor.
NT	If you want to make a pre-auction offer in the Top End, be aware the contract will forgo any cooling off period

2. AT AUCTION

This is the most obvious option, of course. Sometimes it's unavoidable, at other times it's actually in a buyer's best interests to go to auction. The main benefit for buyers is transparency – you can clearly see where your competition is and hear what they're prepared to pay. It's also the neatest and quickest way to negotiate because of the short time lag between having your offer accepted (if you are the highest bidder and the reserve price has been achieved) and signing the contract of sale.

3. AFTER AUCTION

Properties pass in for a number of different reasons. It could be due to a lack of bidders. Or it could be because the owner has set the reserve price too high. It could also be because the agent hasn't managed the marketing campaign very well.

Knowing whether a property has a chance of passing in can be very valuable to a buyer. Sometimes it can be smart to wait for it to pass in and then negotiate afterwards, particularly when the owner needs a reality check.

PRE-AUCTION OFFERS

WHY WOULD YOU DO IT?

Now you know what it's worth and you've done your checks, it's time to work out whether to make an offer beforehand or decide whether it is best to wait until the auction day.

Many buyers are really scared about going to auction because they fear being outbid or they're just daunted by the prospect of performing in public. Fear is not a good reason for making a pre-auction offer: it will often result in you paying too much or missing out completely.

Generally speaking, I make a pre-auction offer when I am confident that the property will sell for more if it gets to auction. The reasoning goes like this: there are a lot of buyers interested in this property, the agent has been quoting a figure that is very attractive to buyers, we know the property worth a lot more because we've done the research, we're ready to buy and it's the right time in the campaign to give our clients an advantage. The secret is to make the offer strong enough to give the vendors pause; they must be unwilling to take the risk of getting less if they go to auction.

MARKET CONDITIONS

Auction clearance rates

Auction clearance rates are used as a measure for determining whether it's a buyers' market or a sellers' market. It stands to reason that auctions are more competitive in a sellers' market and less so in a buyers' market.

The auction clearance rate refers to the percentage of property that has been offered for sale by auction (and the results measured) in a particular week that sold either prior to auction, at auction, or immediately after the auction. So it doesn't purely refer to properties that actually sold 'under the hammer.'

Why does this matter? Well, people tend to assume that all the properties included in the clearance rate sold competitively. But if a property is sold by negotiation after passing in, it probably wasn't competitive. Similarly, if it sold prior to auction there wasn't necessarily more than one buyer. It also relies on vendors setting realistic reserves and agents effectively managing their price expectations.

When the market is truly hot agents are not at all keen to sell prior to auction. However, when the market starts to cool, the first thing we notice is that agents are open to pre-auction offers. These sales are included in the clearance rates, so they could be bolstering the figures while actually masking a softening in the market.

If the agent is encouraging you to make a pre-auction offer, that's a signal that they may not have a lot of other buyers interested in the property. I'll cover the signs to look for in the next section.

CASE STUDY

Maria and Kate were looking to downsize from a big house into an apartment. They found one that they loved that was being quoted at $940,000. After speaking with the agent about making an offer before auction, they were advised that other buyers had indicated around $1.06M. Maria and Kate didn't want to miss out on this one so they decided to put in a strong offer just over $1.1M. This might have bought it, had there not been at least three other buyers prepared to pay similar money. In the end, they secured it before auction for $1.125M – and believe it or not, there were still two other buyers who were prepared to pay more! The reason Maria and Kate were able to buy it was that they started with an offer well over what was being quoted and once pre-auction negotiations begin, the agent is committed to selling the property. Those two other buyers had been caught unawares and weren't ready to sign the contract, so the agent and vendor decided to close the deal with Maria and Kate.

If the agent is discouraging you from making an offer, that is a sign that they have a lot of interest. Under these circumstances, trying to buy the property prior to auction might be the best approach, but be prepared to experience resistance from the agent. A word of caution: if the agent is actively going to work against you, don't do it. There is little to be achieved by getting them offside.

Apart from rare situations where the vendor has instructed the selling agent not to entertain pre-auction offers, there is a very compelling reason for agents to discourage offers. If an offer is rejected, they might have to increase their price guide! They do not want to do this for fear of not being able to build interest and create a competitive auction.

To give you an example, let's say an agent is quoting a property at $900,000. You make an offer of $950,000, which the vendor rejects. The agent now needs to increase their quoting to reflect the fact that the vendor will not accept anything up to and including $950,000. Perhaps that will turn other buyers off, so you can see that making an offer prior to auction can also be a tactical move.

WHEN TO STRIKE

You've found the house of your dreams, you want to buy it, the agent seems receptive, you make an offer ...

And then nothing happens. You are in the dark and getting frustrated. Is your offer accepted or not? Has the agent even given it to the vendor? Are they using it to get another buyer to make a higher offer?

All these thoughts have gone through the minds of property buyers who find themselves in this situation. And it happens more often than you might think. You see, what these buyers don't realise is that there is a hell of a lot of preparation that goes into determining exactly the right time to make an offer. If the agent isn't taking you seriously, you aren't going to get the outcome you desire.

Firstly, you need to get yourself ready to buy. There is no point making an offer until you are ready to sign an unconditional contract (without a cooling off period and not subject to finance, building inspection, sale of another property, etc.) and close the deal.

CASE STUDY

Matt and Dave were keen on a stunning, newly built, architect-designed home. The finishes were cutting edge and it was perfect for entertaining, with an amazing kitchen, beautiful terrace and wet-edge pool. The problem was that the house had been advertised for auction without a complete contract of sale. There are so many documents that need to be signed off, not the least being the home owners warranty certificate, occupation certificate and registration of the subdivision. It seemed that the builders had jumped the gun and failed to anticipate how long the required documentation would take, so effectively the property should not have been offered for sale. Even if a price could be agreed, they didn't have a contract so Matt and Dave couldn't actually buy the property.

Not realising this, they had not only made one offer, they had a couple of their friends make lower offers in order to make their 'real' offer look good. This backfired because the agent and vendor simply got excited about all the interest in the property and their expectations rose as a result.

Not knowing what to do next, they engaged me to help them. In the end it took two weeks for the contract to be finalised and it was only ready on the day before the auction. At least Matt and Dave had not made their best offer earlier in the piece, so we could go to auction with our cards still held close to our chest.

Secondly, understand the auction process. Most auction campaigns run for three weeks of open houses and the auction is held on the final week. The first week is usually too soon to make an offer. The owner and the agent like to feel like they have had enough buyers through the door before they could consider an offer. The last week is often too late to make an offer because other interested buyers are likely to be ready to compete with you.

The optimum time to make a pre-auction offer is in the middle week of the campaign. The agent will feel like they've tested the market and you're more likely to catch other buyers unawares.

PREPARATION CHECKLIST

1. Get your finance pre-approved

2. Research your area and inspect as many properties as possible

3. Do your price research and decide on your maximum bid

4. Complete your due diligence

5. Get the contract reviewed

6. Have your deposit ready

HOW TO DO IT

The best way to make an offer is to be willing and ready to sign a contract ASAP. Ideally you would present your offer on a signed contract! This will ensure that your offer is taken seriously by both the agent and the vendor. It will also limit the opportunity for another less prepared buyer to compete with you.

If you buy prior to auction, you will still need to buy under auction conditions. No agent wants to kill the momentum of an auction campaign by taking the property off the market for five or so days while the buyer gets ready to sign on the dotted line. If the buyer backs out of the deal for any reason, their auction campaign has been ruined.

Once again, the rules are different in every state. For example, in Queensland you can waive the cooling off period without needing to get advice from a solicitor while in NSW, your solicitor needs to issue a 66W Certificate before you can waive your rights to a cooling off period. In Victoria you can only buy without a cooling off period in the three days either side of the auction date, so agents are understandably reticent to accept offers any earlier than those last three days. You will need to have done all of your due diligence and have your finance sorted before you will able to exchange contracts and take the property off the market.

Now all this is a bit dry and unexciting – but if you get the timing wrong here you could cost yourself thousands of dollars. Or worse still, you could lose the property all together.

Say the property you want has a price guide of $1.3M. What this really means is that they want more than $1.3M and the agent might have suggested as high as $1.43M to the owner. If the property goes to auction and the best offer they get is $1.3M, maybe they will sell for that price – but there is no guarantee that they will. For a buyer to buy this property prior to auction, they need to make an offer that will entice the vendor to sell before the auction – as all vendors hope to get competition that will give them a price over their reserve.

As a starting point, I'd expect that they would be thinking at least $1.35M to sell prior to auction. But if there are other interested buyers, this figure will climb. Remember to do your own price research and decide on your walk-away price before even considering an offer.

It's important to recognise that not all agents employ the same negotiation tactics. How the agent is managing their vendor's expectations is a crucial factor to consider. Some agents are desperate to get you to make an offer because they need one in order to 'condition' their owner. In these circumstances your offer is unlikely to buy the property and often you'll get no feedback for days. Some agents will try to call your bluff by talking about some nebulous 'other buyer' and their vague offer. However, an agent who is about to sell a property is usually very clear with their instructions to a prospective buyer, because those who are dealing with serious buyers and a motivated vendor won't muck around.

With some agents you have to give a low offer first as they won't know how to present a decent offer to their vendor. Really inexperienced agents can fall into this category, or really bad, unprofessional ones. By starting off at a figure less than what you are prepared to go to you will be conditioning the vendor and allowing the agent to look like they are negotiating. When you get to the point of submitting your final offer, the vendor will be better prepared to recognise it for what it is and hopefully accept it.

Sometimes, when you're dealing with an agent like this, it's simpler to go to auction.

Is the agent likely to work with you on this or are they likely to be difficult to deal with? Before you make your offer, ask the agent how they handle pre-auction offers, because if they say to you that they are going to 'shop it around' so that every buyer knows what every other buyer has offered, then you potentially are going to end up in a blind-auction scenario. You'll be on the end of the telephone, where you can't see or hear how high those other buyers are prepared to go to. You'd be better off going to auction under those circumstances.

If, however, the agent is keen to work with you and is going to give you some set parameters and clear guidance around their process, then making an offer prior to auction will be more straightforward.

But a word of warning: be careful if they're too eager. You might be better to go to auction because you could be paying too much if you offer first.

EXAMPLES OF AGENT 'RULES OF ENGAGEMENT'

- Offers to be submitted on a contract by 5pm the following day.
- With each offer they'll let every interested buyer know what price they have to beat. The last one standing will be the buyer.
- Offers to be submitted in writing, with all terms noted by 2pm the following day. The successful bidder will be notified and given till 5pm to present their signed contract and deposit cheque to the agent.

Once your offer is accepted, close the deal as soon as possible. Get your signed unconditional contract and deposit cheque to the agent and ideally wait in their office until they confirm the property is yours!

CASE STUDY

Justin had been looking for his first apartment for nine months and he felt like he was always losing out at auction to investors who had more money. When he found another unit that he really liked, the sales agent suggested that he make an offer prior to the auction and that he'd guide him through the process. Justin followed his advice, step by step, right up to the point where he gave the agent a signed contract. He thought at this stage that the property was his. What he didn't realise was that the agent needed to notify all the other interested buyers that the property was about to be sold. One of those buyers was able to move quickly and also sign a contract that same day, for more money. Justin was then faced with the choice of increasing his offer or missing out. He was so dismayed and angry that he stood his ground and the other buyer bought it.

There are two lessons we can learn from Justin's experience. The first is that before he gave the agent the contract he should have checked on the process the agent would follow and ideally given the offer with a deadline to close the deal. The second is that if Justin had a crystal clear idea of how much the property was really worth, he might have been confident enough to increase his offer rather than freeze because he thought he was being ripped off.

PRE-AUCTION OFFER CHECKLIST

1. Market conditions

In a hot market, it might be a good idea to consider trying to buy before auction, because if you wait until the auction, there's likely to be a lot of competition and you will have a higher chance of being outbid. But in a slower market, you could end up being the only buyer there or the other buyers may not want to compete that hard. You might actually do better by going to auction.

2. What is the property worth?

If you think the property is worth a lot more than the agent is quoting, then you might have a good opportunity to buy prior because your offer, based on what you know it's worth, will sound very attractive to both the agent and the owner. Since you've done your research you'll know that if it gets to auction, it's likely that you will have to pay even more. Just make sure your offer is strong enough to get a quick answer from the agent and then sign the contract ASAP. However, if the agent is quoting a price and you think the property is worth around the same or maybe even a little less, then you have nothing to gain by making an offer prior to auction. You're going to do better by going to auction.

3. What's the agent like?

Some agents will have a very clear process and they will explain exactly what happens, others will bumble and fluff around. When an agent bumbles and fluffs, you're going to have to take control or just go to auction. But when dealing with agents who have a clear process, don't try and buck the system. Follow their instructions because trying to be smart is not going to win you any favours.

4. Are you ready to sign a contract?

If it looks like making an offer prior to auction is a good idea, then you need to be fully prepared before you submit that offer. You'll need to be ready to buy the property under auction conditions. Do all of your due diligence and, when you make that offer, be prepared to hand over a signed contract with your deposit. Lastly, give the agent a deadline and let them know you'll be back to collect the contract if they don't finalise the deal.

WHAT IF ANOTHER BUYER MAKES AN OFFER?

Once again, the laws differ from state to state. In most circumstances, if a pre-auction offer has been accepted on a property but contracts have not yet been exchanged, then other buyers are free to submit offers. This is especially true when making an offer prior to auction. There is no law in place to make agents respond to a competitive offer in any set way, which means that you can't be certain how the selling agent will react if it happens to you. Some will freely share information amongst buyers so you will all know the amount each buyer has offered, whereas others will be more discreet. Some will favour the original buyer while others only care about the highest sale price. Some will keep shopping around for increased offers until the buyers are all exhausted, others will give a deadline for best and final offers in a sealed envelope.

Generally speaking, one of three things is likely to happen if another buyer tries to gazump you:

1. The vendor decides to honour your original agreement (at the lower price),

2. the vendor gives you the first right of refusal at the higher price, or

3. they accept the higher offer. And if they accept the offer, the whole scenario could happen again if you or another buyer steps in with an even higher offer.

This is where it's critical that you set your maximum bid before you start negotiations. Don't deviate from this. If you have room to negotiate, then by all means increase your offer. If you don't, walk away. There will always be another property.

If you increase your bid, you will then still need to race to get your signed contract to the agent as another buyer could still match or better your offer. Depending on whether the selling agent discloses offers or not, this could be a good strategy as the vendor may treat you more favourably – though there are no guarantees.

The best way to avoid all of this is to make sure that you are ready to sign an unconditional contract *before* you make an offer. Closing the gap between when you make your offer and when you actually buy the property will give less opportunity for other buyers to step in.

If you are the buyer who wants to gazump another, you have to make a serious offer designed to entice the vendors to renege on their previous agreement – don't just add a couple of thousand dollars to the price. And if your offer is accepted, you in turn had better move quickly to avoid being gazumped ...

Sealed bids

When there is a lot of interest in a property it is not uncommon for the sales agent to call for 'best and final' offers. This is usually a 'sealed bid' scenario. The downside is that it is 'sudden death' and the upside is that offers don't get shopped around to all buyers.

It's hard going in blind, so here are a couple of pointers to help.

Ask the agent the following:

1. What sort of price have buyers been indicating and where do you need to be in order to buy it? The agent may not answer but they might. In the absence of guidance you will need to rely solely on your own price assessment.

2. What is their process after their offer deadline? Do they expect the offers to be in writing? Or on a signed contract? If they are accepting written offers by the deadline, how long do you have before they expect a signed contract from the highest bidder?

CASE STUDY

Adam and Rebecca were first-home buyers looking to buy a house to renovate. Adam was an electrician, with loads of tradie mates and Rebecca was doing a part-time interior design course. They found a great little 'doer-upper': an old worker's cottage on a level block of land. It was run down but looked to be structurally sound, so they imagined they'd be able to live in it while they renovated. They were so keen they wanted to jump straight in with an offer. My recommendation was to wait until they had all the information on the property. Now, the results of the building and pest inspection showed more asbestos than expected, so our buyers got an expert in to quote on the removal, which came in at a whopping $40,000, drastically altering the price they would be prepared to pay. Imagine trying to get the vendor's expectations down that far if they thought they had already done a deal at a higher price.

WHY, WHEN AND HOW REAL ESTATE AGENTS TRY TO GET YOU TO MAKE AN OFFER BEFORE AUCTION

If the sales agent is encouraging you to make an offer before auction, then it's probably *not* in your best interests to do so.

When the market is hot, agents are less likely to encourage you to make an offer before auction. This is because they know they'll get competition and it will sell on the day – it doesn't matter to them who buys the property. They also know that a pre-auction offer could start a messy bidding war, at the end of which, they'll have a number of disgruntled buyers on their hands. The agent doesn't want to look bad. They would much prefer to go to auction and have you blame the other buyers if you miss out, not them.

When the market slows down, we see sales agents encouraging buyers to make an offers. This is because they are worried about the outcome of the auction. They are not confident that any or all of the interested buyers will turn up and bid. They think that one buyer is probably stronger than all the others and so they want to flush this buyer out.

Be wary if the agent advises you that somebody else has made an offer and it looks like it's going to sell prior. Note that 'it *might* sell prior.' Some agents go on a fishing expedition and try to get you on the hook. If this happens, ask specific questions:

1. Has the vendor accepted an offer?

2. Is it definitely going to sell before the auction?

3. When is the deadline for receiving an unconditional offer?

4. What process are you going to follow?

5. How much information will you disclose to each interested party?

CASE STUDY

Sally called me on a Monday. She was keen on a house that was going to auction the following Thursday. The agent had been on the phone and told her that 'another buyer has made an offer and the owner would like to sell it but this buyer wants a six-month settlement.' Sally fell into the trap and made an offer of $1.25M. Almost immediately she realised she was out of her depth and she called me.

As soon as I heard her story and the things the sales agent had been saying, I suspected that Sally was the only buyer. When agents are vague about the details of other buyers, their offers and exactly when they think the property will be sold, I start to suspect that they are trying to bluff a buyer into making an offer. I encouraged Sally to cool her heels. Then I let the agent know that she was serious and we needed to do all the due diligence so she'd be ready to bid in four days' time.

The agent was not happy, but he didn't have a choice. My instincts were right: Sally was the only buyer he had. We went to auction, we let it pass in and negotiated with the agent in their offices. It took over an hour, but we secured that property for $50,000 less than Sally had offered on the Monday.

Usually these approaches are made by agents in the final week of their campaign. By this stage they know if there is only one serious buyer and their owner has lost hope of having a competitive auction.

Example 1:

The agent calls, *'I have a buyer coming in today with an offer that the vendor will probably accept. But they are also putting an offer on another property and they'll buy whichever one gets accepted first. I really think this property will sell today, so I encourage you to put your best foot forward so you don't miss out.'*

Our clients were still in two minds about this property and didn't feel the need to make an offer before auction, so we decided to call the agent's bluff. Sure enough, it didn't sell and the auction was cancelled. The agent gave himself a 'get out of jail free card' by saying the buyer had made offers on two properties. In this way, he felt he wouldn't have egg on his face in the event that the property didn't actually sell as he has predicted. We bought it a few days later at a price less than he was pushing for prior to auction.

Example 2:

The agent calls, *'A buyer has made an offer over the guide price that is acceptable to the vendor except that there is a condition attached that is not appealing to them. However, they will sell the property to them today unless another buyer comes in with a more attractive offer. I am meeting them at 12 pm, so I need your best offer in by then and they will sell.'* We heard this similar story only a week after the last one, once again the day before the scheduled auction.

In this instance our clients shaped up to put in their best offer, which was also over the guide price. The agent's response was that we were 'miles away'. So we let it go. It didn't sell after all and the agent then indicated a price almost $300,000 higher than her original price. This agent didn't provide a face-saving pre-emptive explanation for a non-sale. Instead she clearly demonstrated to us that the vendor had high price expectations and she had no buyers interested anywhere near that level.

Both of these agents worked to elicit buyers to make an offer before auction because they knew it wasn't going to be competitive. It takes a lot of nerve to call an agent's bluff (especially if you really want the property) but it's important to realise that agents will encourage offers if their campaign isn't going that well. If they have lots of buyers, they'd always prefer to go to auction.

If you want to learn more about how and when agents manufacture offers prior to auction, there are plenty of examples in *The Elephant in the Room* property podcast. You can listen to the specific episodes via this link: www.getauctionready.com.au/bonus.

CHAPTER 7

AUCTION DAY: BUYING PROPERTY AT AUCTION

GET PREPARED AND GIVE YOURSELF A STRATEGIC ADVANTAGE

You've done a lot of the preparation already. You've completed all of your due diligence and you're very clear on what your maximum bid will be. Your finance is approved and you know how you'll be paying the deposit. You have your contract changes agreed to and you're ready to go!

Not quite so fast. There's quite a bit to learn about what to expect at the auction and I also want to ensure that you are feeling as calm as possible.

Make sure you are well rested and do not go out on the town the night before. I can't tell you how many hungover bidders I've seen and they weren't thinking clearly. Your judgement is affected when you're under the weather as is your ability to resist an agent who asks you to increase your bid.

I don't recommend taking a support crew. Family and friends can be a comfort but also a distraction. You may be tempted to perform for your audience. And don't take the kids! You need to be laser-focussed during the auction.

Before the auction, check in with yourself one last time about your maximum bid. Does it still sit well with you? Are you still OK paying that price? If another buyer pays $1,000 more, will you be happy to walk away? Make sure you are committed to the limit you set yourself.

In some states you will have to register in order to be able to bid, so take your ID (driver's licence is fine) and your cheque book, unless you've made arrangements for a bank transfer into the agent's trust account.

If the auction is to be held on-site there will usually be an inspection for half an hour prior, so make sure you get there early to get a gauge on how many people are likely to bid. Watch the other bidders as they register. If the auction is to be held in-rooms, you won't necessarily be able to do this, though I still suggest you get there early.

When the bidding starts, you want to position yourself where you can see other bidders and watch their body language. This is much more important than watching the auctioneer.

❗ AUCTION PREPARATION CHECKLIST

- ☐ Find a babysitter for the kids
- ☐ Get a good night's sleep
- ☐ Don't have a hangover
- ☐ Don't take your entire family
- ☐ Last pressure test of your maximum bid
- ☐ Don't forget your cheque book & ID
- ☐ Get there early
- ☐ Watch the registrations

If you have any niggling doubts about the property, DO NOT GO TO THE AUCTION. I have seen people buy some pretty ordinary houses because the agent was very clever at getting them to bid even though they were in two minds about it.

SIX TIPS TO HELP YOU CALM YOUR NERVES IN A HOT AUCTION MARKET:

1. Remember that auctions might be scary but there are some benefits to buyers: transparency being the biggest.

2. Don't assume that all agents underquote by the same ratio or amount.

3. Do your own research on recent comparable sales and make up your own mind about a reasonable market price for the property.

4. Don't make a pre-auction offer simply because you fear competition. Remember that you need to make a really strong offer which needs to be well in excess of other buyer interest at the time.

5. Don't make a pre-auction offer unless you are ready to sign a contract under auction conditions.

6. Set your limit before you go to auction, not during the auction. Ask yourself at what point you would kick yourself if someone else bought it.

THE PSYCHOLOGY OF REAL ESTATE AUCTIONS

I've always been fascinated by human behaviour and, in particular, understanding why property buyers do the things they do. As much as we like to think we make rational decisions, the reality is that the subconscious, emotional part of our brain is actually a hell of a lot bigger than the rational part and therefore controls us most of the time.

Auctions influence our subconscious mind in many ways. Some are a result of deliberate strategies employed by the agent and/or auctioneer; other ways are by virtue of the auction process itself. Auctions are stressful. Making significant purchasing decisions is complicated. We take mental shortcuts when confronted with big, complex decision-making, and what could be bigger and more complex than competing at an auction? This isn't just me saying so, these effects have been studied by behavioural scientists. (Check out Nobel Prize-winner Daniel Kahneman's book: *Thinking Fast and Slow.*)

Awareness is the first step in being able to take charge and not let your subconscious mind rule the show. I'm a co-host of a podcast called *The Elephant in the Room*. The elephant is a metaphor for our subconscious mind and the rider is our rational mind (*The Happiness Hypothesis* by Jonathan Haidt, Basic Books, 2006). It doesn't take a great deal of imagination to see who is really in charge of direction. Most of us think that we are rational creatures who are making informed decisions but the science shows that our subconscious mind has greater influence over our rational mind than the opposite.

Throughout this book you will find strategies to help you overcome the pull of the 'elephant.' Having awareness is good first step, but it's important to have strategies to keep you focussed on your rational decision-making and thought processes.

12 behavioural biases that can be activated during an auction. See how many you identify with.

Reciprocity effect

Ever seen a coffee cart or gelato van outside a house that's about to go under the hammer? It's not there purely for your enjoyment. The elephant feels an obligation to give something in return for a gift. This return doesn't have to be proportionate, so a bid in exchange for a cafe latte isn't out of the question.

I'm not saying that you shouldn't take the coffee but I am saying that you should be aware that you might feel a subtle pull to return the favour in some small way. Just notice this and realise you can resist!

Scarcity effect

We value things when they are perceived to be scarce. In real estate this can be a good thing, properties that are rare and in demand can be great investments. The issue here is that the sense of scarcity can be manufactured. Pay attention to the things the auctioneer might say about this 'unique opportunity.' Auctioneers also work hard to create urgency throughout the auction and will get their gavel out and call 'going once, going twice, going ...' to make it sound like time is running out even when the reserve has not been met. This is a deliberate tactic designed to get you to bid!

Make no mistake, guarding yourself against these tactics is really difficult. Even I feel the pull of FOMO (fear of missing out) and, let's face it, I have 20 years' experience under my belt, thorough knowledge of the value of the property I'm bidding for and it's not my money! The best way to prepare yourself for this is to witness as many auctions as you can before you bid. You'll start to see subtle changes between the 'going once, twice, three times' of a bluff versus when the property really is about to be sold. One tip I can give you: the first time the auctioneer raises their gavel is usually a bluff.

Anchoring

Anchoring is a tactic some auctioneers use to draw our expectations towards the vendor's expected price. The auctioneer uses this to effectively get everyone on the same page. Have you ever gone to an auction where there is a crowd and the room is buzzing? If you intend to bid on that property, your anxiety tends to rise in accordance with the amount of other people who also seem keen. You're already probably thinking you have to increase your limit. And then the auctioneer suggests a figure that's a bit higher again.

Like it or not, you are going to be affected by anchoring, so be on the lookout for it. You might hear a phrase like 'houses in this street have been selling for around a million dollars' when actually the agent has only been quoting $850,000 for the one being auctioned. Or it could be that the auctioneer seeks to get bidding started at a higher price and then quickly drops the suggested opening bid.

The auctioneer will also use anchoring to get you to bid in different increments. For example, they may start off by suggesting $20,000 bids. You don't have to follow their lead. Of course, they may reject your bid if it's too low but if nobody else bids, they'll come back to you.

Once again, awareness is step one. When you have thoroughly researched market value and are clear on your maximum bid you are less likely to be swayed by the auctioneer's suggestions.

Loss aversion

We fear loss because the pain of losing is more intense than the joy of winning. So when the auctioneer frames things in a way that emphasises the downside, you are going to be influenced to bid. For instance, they could say, 'Imagine how good you'll feel this afternoon if you're the highest bidder?' but a more powerful way to phrase that would be, 'Do you want to admit to your friends that you let this property go for $1,000?' Watch out for this one next time you're at auction, it's subtle.

When we focus on one property to the exclusion of all others we are at greater risk of falling prey to loss aversion. It's important to retain perspective. Be clear on the likelihood of whether another property like this will come up again in a reasonable time period. The more familiar you are with the market in which you are buying, the better equipped you will be to answer this question.

Sunk cost

Once you have spent money, you should remove it from your decision-making. Just because you've paid for a building and pest inspection and conveyancing doesn't mean that you should bid over your limit. People do though.

Tackling this one takes discipline. You really do have to draw a line and say to yourself: 'That money has gone, whether I buy this property or not.' The most important thing is to buy the right property at the right price.

Recency effect

We tend to be influenced by what is vivid and tangible, and recent experiences have an impact. Of course, when it comes to real estate, this can swing both ways. In a booming market we all assume that what happened at last week's auctions will also happen this week and so we bid with gusto. Of course, the auctioneer will also remind us of these results! In a soft market we do the opposite, often not bidding because we believe prices will fall. Sort of a self-fulfilling prophecy, this one.

Social proof

If someone else thinks it, it must be true. We look around at the crowd, at other people bidding, and we feel reassured. *This is a good property*, we think. *It must be worth this amount of money because other people are bidding.* Of course the opposite also happens and an auctioneer has dialogue that they will use in order to counteract the negative side of this bias. ('Don't be put off by the lack of people here today. There are interested buyers who couldn't get their finance ready before the auction and they'll be making offers next week if we don't sell now.') When you think about it, it's a bit sad that we look to others to ratify such important life decisions. There is no substitute for taking the time to carefully consider what you are buying and the short and long term implications.

Even how crowded or not the auction is can create social proof. We have to make a conscious effort to remind ourselves that everybody else has a reason for either being or not being at that auction. If the agent and vendor have 'rented a crowd,' this does not mean you should automatically be primed to pay more. On the flipside, if the crowd is thin because the agent didn't underquote during the campaign, or because it's held at 9am in the middle of winter, the lack of social proof might cause you to keep your hand in your pocket instead of potentially nabbing a bargain.

Herding

Remember Monty Python's famous quote from the movie, *The Life of Brian*? 'You're all individuals,' says Brian. Then a lone voice says: 'I'm not.' We are influenced by others even if we think we aren't. We like to be part of a group and if the group is buying property, we don't want to be left behind. FOMO during a property boom is the classic example!

Consistency effect

Once you take an action, you feel committed to that course of action. There are different levels of the effect: it increases with the more public the action is as people don't want to appear foolish or be seen to 'go back' on their word. You may feel once you paid for the building and pest inspection or once you have asked for a contract that you must follow through and buy the property. This is not so! You can see how the idea of consistency comes into play once you make one bid. You are much more likely to place a second bid, even if it's over your limit, rather than run the risk of appearing foolish.

The way to combat this is to be certain before you act. If you are not 100 percent committed to buying that property, *do not bid!* If you find yourself in this situation, ask yourself, 'What is more foolish, stopping bidding or buying something I'm not sure I want for more money than I wanted to pay?'

Mental accounting

We all divide our money into different buckets in our minds. We compartmentalise our money so we can justify the way we spend it. More mundane items we often prefer to 'save' on, but we are more willing to spend on more exciting items or items we perceive to be 'an investment.' When you hear the auctioneer talking about what a good investment the property is, they are tapping into this idea of mental accounting.

We are willing to spend more if we have had a windfall or if we can justify 'the investment.' So by couching in terms of investment, even if you are planning to live in the property, the auctioneer is trying to leverage that bucket from which we have more willingness to spend.

If you've recently sold your house and made more money than you expected to, this 'windfall' may also be reflected in your mental accounting. You may spend more at an auction than a property is worth because you feel so cashed-up.

Just remember to separate your ability to pay from what the property is worth. You don't have to over pay just because you can! And if the auctioneer is suggesting it's a good investment – just remember that the property market is unregulated and many agents make this sort of claim with no real basis. Most of them actually have no clue about what makes a good investment – so don't be swayed!

Overconfidence

Some people think they are good at bidding at auction in just the same way that many people think they are good drivers. This type of person often has no idea how bad they actually are and it's magnified if they have previously 'won' at auction. We tend to systematically learn from the things we do well but not so much from the things we got wrong. It's a big risk with some people.

For example, if we are successful in our career, we may fall into the trap of overconfidence in other aspects of our lives (very common with alpha males and c-suite executives). So, it goes to follow that if we have successfully negotiated a couple of property purchases in our lives, we may think we can't go wrong. What happens is that we operate with the underlying assumption that nothing is different this time around. And because we don't effectively know what we don't know, we fools rush in where angels fear to tread. When it comes to buying property, being overconfident can cost hundreds of thousands of dollars. But you'll never know, because you're a good negotiator, right?

This is a particular problem if you find that your partner is overconfident. It's your money they're playing with too, so you've got to find a way to draw their attention to the potential downside!

Overoptimism

We can be vulnerable to media reports, history of growth and perception of continued growth so we might think we can't lose. In a booming market we see this 'elephant' running rampant.

The buyer who thinks they cannot lose on property is prone to paying too much at auction. A classic example is the renovator/flipper who managed to ride the market wave and make a decent profit on their last project. Overoptimism combined with overconfidence can be a potent mix, leading them to pay too much for the wrong property and then over capitalise without paying enough attention to market conditions.

It's really important to remember that property is a risky business and due care must always be taken when making such a major financial commitment.

Source: Behavioural Finance Expert Simon Russell on
The Elephant in the Room, episode 1.

THE RESERVE PRICE, VENDOR BIDS AND WHEN IT IS 'ON THE MARKET'

HOW IS THE RESERVE PRICE SET?

The auctioneer needs the reserve price in writing from the vendor. This is the price below which the property cannot be sold.

In a small percentage of cases, the property is being auctioned following a court order or instructions in a will and the reserve price will be set following a formal valuation. Under these circumstances it is unlikely that the reserve can be adjusted.

In most cases, however, the owner sets the reserve price on the day of the auction and it is completely at their discretion. Note that it is not set in stone and the agent will ask the vendor to reduce it if the auction is not going well. Some encourage their clients to have two reserves – the one they'd like to exceed and the one at which they'll sell if they have to.

Sometimes, in a flagging auction, the agent will show the highest bidder the written reserve in an effort to get them to increase their bid. This is merely a tactic to make you think the vendor will move down and thereby encourage you to increase your bid. You can stay firm and don't need to be moved by it.

If the property passes in, most agents will initially negotiate only with the highest bidder. But this is a courtesy only. They are still free to take offers from anybody.

WHAT IS A VENDOR BID?

A vendor bid is exercised by the auctioneer on the vendor's behalf. In NSW the vendor is allowed one bid. In most other states, including Victoria, they can submit numerous vendor bids.

The auctioneer might use a vendor bid if there are only a few registered bidders or if bidding stops well short of reserve. YOU DO NOT HAVE TO BID HIGHER unless you really think the property is worth it.

DOES THE AUCTIONEER HAVE TO DECLARE THE PROPERTY 'ON THE MARKET'?

The auctioneer will usually try to bluff the audience to think that the property is about to sell even if bidding hasn't hit reserve. They want your hands in the air – not in your pockets as you wait to hear those magical words.

Most auctioneers don't like to call the property 'on the market' once the bidding reaches the reserve price. If buyers are trained to wait for those words, the auctioneer won't be able to call your bluff earlier in the auction to get things moving. They use the 'going once, twice ...' call before the reserve is met to encourage bidding – that's when it's calling the bidders' bluff. So if everyone is waiting for them to say 'it's now on the market', they would never be able to use the 'going once, twice ...' trick.

Be on the lookout for a distinctly different tempo and tone of voice from the auctioneer as a tipoff for when the reserve has been met. When it really is going to sell there is a definite change in the auctioneer's demeanour. This is why it's important to observe plenty of auctions before you go to one to bid: so you can tell the difference between a bluff and the real deal.

CHAPTER 8

BIDDING AT AUCTION

BIDDING TACTICS FOR A WINNING STRATEGY

Barbeque conversations often drift to auction bidding tactics and there's always somebody who thinks they're an expert. There are many common tricks such as a strong opening bid or waiting until the property is 'on the market' before bidding, but they are all a bit predictable. To be successful at auction you'll need a number of battle plans ready to go, depending on what unfolds on the day.

Here are some of the scenarios you could be presented with and will need to have a game plan for:

- It's frantically competitive and you can't seem to get a bid in.

- Nobody else bids, so will you open the bidding and what is the right bid to make?

- The auctioneer places a vendor bid after your bid.

- You're the highest bidder but it's under reserve. When should you let the property pass in and negotiate?

- You want to make an offer less than the vendor bid.

- The agent shows you the written reserve. What does it mean?

- If the agent tells you the reserve, do you believe them?

- The agent won't tell you the reserve. Does that mean it's ridiculously high?

- Will the highest bidder have exclusive rights to negotiate after auction?

- Other buyers want to make offers after the property passed in.

- When is it better to negotiate with the agent before the hammer falls and when is it better to let the property pass in?

- How can you get the owner to lower their reserve price?

There are a number of bidding tactics that you can employ but you need to recognise that every auction is different and no one tactic will apply every time.

THE KNOCK-OUT BID

Sometimes, a slam-dunk bid can work wonders – especially if it's the opening bid. You just have to be quite brave but also very, very calculating in how you do it. Understanding what the property is worth is key to the success of this tactic.

A knock-out bid is useful when there are loads of registered bidders and the agent has been underquoting. Start the bidding at what you think the property is worth in order to blow your competition out of the water. This can be very effective, though it's not failsafe.

If buyers are nervous about the market, they are going to seek reassurance from the bidding of other buyers. A knock-out bid can work well if used during the auction in these circumstances. A buyer is more likely to exceed their maximum budget once they get into the momentum of the auction. They're less likely to go over their limit if the bidding hasn't really started. If you can make it so that the auction never gets off the ground because you've already hit the big number, you could stop a bidding war taking off and secure the property for what you know to be a fair amount (due to your research, of course).

The knock-out bid is designed to do what its name suggests: knock out the competition. So, let's say you are prepared to pay $900,000 for a property and people are bidding competitively and have reached the low $800,000s. It won't take many $10,000 bids before your limit is blown. So why not disrupt the momentum of the auction with a bold bid at your maximum amount? It can be very effective and will work sometimes. Other times, after a collective gasp, a really serious buyer (or two) manages to recover and knock you out. So only do this if you think the property is worth it and if you are confident that competitive bidding could take the price even higher.

Of course, bidding strong can have some drawbacks. You may manage to scare off other buyers but you may also encourage the vendor with a high reserve to leave it high. For example, some vendors need to see competitive bidding before they feel they've achieved market value. If only one bid was made, they might justify to themselves that there weren't enough serious buyers at the auction instead of accepting that the strongest buyer scared everyone else off. The agent has very little ammunition to argue the case with an owner who chooses this interpretation.

AGGRESSION

You only bid aggressively at auction if you want to scare off other buyers, so you have to be confident that there is serious competition for you to beat.

A great tactic is to stare down your opposition with a wry smile. A confident stance can do wonders in out-psyching other bidders and making them think you have bottomless pockets. We see many would-be buyers stop bidding prematurely because they believe the other bidders will stop at nothing.

FIVE AGGRESSIVE BIDDING SCENARIOS

1. **You have more money than everybody else.**
   And you don't care what you have to pay.

2. **You know what that property is worth.**
   You also know that the agent has been severely under-quoting it, so you could come in really aggressively and scare off quite a lot of other buyers who have wishful thinking and are hoping that the property is going to sell at a much lower price.

3. **When you're bidding against inexperienced bidders.**
   By bidding aggressively you can easily scare them off.

4. **When the market is hot and you want to scare off as many other bidders as possible in one hit.**

5. **In a cooler market but where there are a lot of registered bidders.**

Be careful though, bidding aggressively against another aggressive bidder is a recipe for disaster. When you lock horns with another competitive bidder it's easy to forget about the value of the property, as you're actually just competing to win. What you need to do is disarm them.

Fundamentally, bidding aggressively is all about control. You're wanting to control the auction, and there are some other methods you can employ to achieve that.

BIDDING INCREMENTS

An auctioneer wants to create a rhythm, so disruptive bidding can be quite effective in changing the pace of an auction. You could try asking questions during the auction (this is one for the extrovert who is prepared to be unpopular) or engaging the auctioneer in some humorous banter, or bid in odd numbers and increments (only try this if you are good with numbers) or even bid twice in quick succession (this really puts people off!).

Being politely disruptive is one of my personal favourites. When you mix up the bidding increments you really disarm bidders (and sometimes the auctioneer also!). People aren't expecting that, they're expecting the bidding to start in bigger numbers and slowly go down until it gets to the pointy end, so I like to mess it up a little bit. One of my favourite tactics is to use odd numbers and chop and change the increments. So, I might make a $13,000 bid, then an $8,000 bid then a $17,000 bid. Once I even asked each other bidder to show me the number on their bidder's paddle and then I matched them in my bids. So, after bidder number 9, I bid $9,000, after bidder number 13, I bid $13,000, and so on. It certainly keeps people guessing!

Another tactic is bidding before you're asked to by the auctioneer, or you could offer a higher number than you've been asked for. After all, if you know it's below the reserve it doesn't really matter what the bidding increment is at this point. So if the auctioneer asks you for $25,000 bid, why not give them $30,000? Other buyers will find it hard to work out what to make of that.

BIDDING AGAINST YOURSELF

Another slightly crazy tactic is to bid against yourself. Sometimes I'll increase my own bid and people think I'm insane. It results in the other bidders having to stop and think before their next move.

CASE STUDY

The first time I saw a buyer bid against himself, I thought it was one of the most interesting auction bidding tactics I'd ever encountered. He certainly scared off at least one buyer in the process. He pushed in with a bid and then confused the auctioneer by almost immediately raising his own bid by $10,000. The auctioneer didn't know where that bid came from and then when he realised it came from the same guy, he tried to refuse to take the bid (interesting move, given that bidding had passed the reserve price). So the buyer upped his bid again by another $10,000! When the auctioneer rejected that bid also, he spoke up and added another $2,000 and clearly stated that he was prepared to pay that figure for this property. He certainly stalled the auction for a moment and I think more than one buyer thought 'I am not going to bid against that mad man.' In the end, another bidder did take him on and after a few more bids the crazy double-bidder finally won the property.

Consider this: how many other auction bidding tactics like this could be used instead of a knock-out bid? What's the difference between making a bold $25,000 bid or a succession of five $5,000 bids? Would that be more effective in scaring off would-be buyers?

WAITING

The most popular tactic amongst inexperienced bidders seems to be to wait until it's 'on the market'. This is my least favourite tactic because you really hand control of the auction over to the auctioneer and other bidders.

What is the point in waiting until the property is called 'on the market' to bid? How is it ever going to reach reserve unless people bid? Plenty of properties sell under the reserve at auction after a bit of frantic negotiation between agent and vendor. And not all auctioneers will call the property 'on the market', so you need to be careful if you've decided to wait instead of bidding earlier.

DON'T BID

Of course, you always have the option not to bid. If you are the only registered bidder, you can opt to negotiate with the agent directly and not go through the charade of an auction.

Once you commit to bidding, give it all you've got. Timid bidding just leaves the door open for other timid buyers to have a crack. When you get close to your limit, stick to your game plan. Don't give the game away. Don't look to your partner for reassurance. Don't discuss whether you should increase your limit. These are all invitations to other bidders to keep bidding.

Good auctioneers these days are trained to deal with hecklers and arrogant bidders, so the best way to put your stamp on an auction is to be charming and unpredictable.

Most of the time it is true that those with the deepest pockets will end up buying the property but it is not always the case and if you can take control of the auction, or, at least, disrupt the flow, you can have an impact on the overall outcome.

In the unlikely event that all bidders have the same limit, it becomes a race to the finish and the first one there will get to buy the property.

UNDERSTANDING YOUR OPPONENTS: THE DIFFERENT TYPES OF BIDDERS

Bidding at auction, particularly real estate auctions, can be terrifying, especially if you have your heart set on buying the property. The fear is heightened in a hot market when prices are rising almost on a daily basis.

Many buyers, left to their own devices get scared off by aggressive bidders and stop bidding prematurely. Many others get caught up in the adrenalin created by a competitive auction and end up bidding well above their limit. Plenty of people think they have the perfect auction-winning strategy and end up shaking their heads as others with their own winning tactics overtake them.

I have been to hundreds (possibly thousands) of auctions in my time and find it fascinating to watch different bidding tactics. Auctions can be stressful for everyone involved and often buyers surprise themselves: by either bidding more or less than they thought they would. Some buyers register for auctions and never even end up bidding (which I do find odd ...). Others get caught up in the emotion and seem to forget about what they are even bidding for.

There are five particular types of people who can be formidable opponents at auction. It's a good idea to be aware of these in the event that you ever come across one because they will either pay too much for the property or they will make sure someone else does. If you take on these bidders you'll probably overpay, which is why you need to have set your uppermost limit before you go to auction and do not go over it.

THE BANK OF MUM AND DAD

Baby Boomer (or even older Gen X) parents are keen to get their Gen Y offspring on the property ladder. Their numbers rose in the recent property boom, driven by the increase in value of their own homes. After registering for auction, it is usually Dad holding the bidder's card. Sometimes they are a little smug because they know that their kid has an advantage over any poor first-home buyer without parental help. When the bidding gets to high levels, Dad often continues 'because he can.' I've even seen sons and daughters trying to stop their fathers to no avail. This is one very emotional bidder indeed!

THE TESTOSTERONE BIDDER

I think we can see a bit of a pattern here, for this is another male bidder. The alpha male bids with a 'win at all costs' attitude. This buyer hates to lose, but the paradox is that in bidding the way they do, they do in fact lose something: they lose sight of what they are actually buying! This bidder is difficult to take on because, in the moment, they don't seem to worry about affordability.

You might be interested to know that auctioneers love these types of bidders. They know that they are prone to overconfidence, which often leads to overpaying.

THE SELLING AGENT BIDDING FOR THEIR CLIENT

Some buyers ask their friendly sales agent to bid for them because they are not confident with auctions. It makes sense: their agent is an expert (at selling property, though, not buying) but often they are overconfident at auction. I know this from experience as I had to 'untrain' myself when I switched from being a selling agent to a buyer's agent.

Selling agents often bid for their clients when they know that there is a new listing in it for them. There is a bit of a conflict of interest here, because obviously they want their client to be the ultimate buyer. Consequently, there is unlikely to be any critical analysis of what the property is actually worth.

It's in the DNA of a sales agent to think that being the highest bidder is the best outcome. They tend to believe that they need to bid hard and high and knock out all the other buyers. Sometimes this is an appropriate tactic, but these bidders tend to use the same approach every time they bid.

The only good thing about coming up against one of these bidders is that they should have a written limit, but if their client is with them (or on the phone), they may encourage them to exceed it.

THE BIDDER WHO JUST MISSED OUT

This buyer is still licking their wounds from the auction they missed out on only last week. They are full of regret over 'the one that got away' and in their forensic review of that auction they have determined that they need to bid harder next time. They'll do whatever it takes as they don't want to miss out again, they really want to avoid reliving that pain.

THE BUYER WHO JUST SOLD

When someone has just sold their home (without first buying their next one) they are immediately faced with the option of renting until they find a new home to buy or buying something ASAP and avoiding a double move. The weeks immediately after their sale are when the pressure is greatest on this buyer. Their defences are down and they are most likely to compromise in ways they would never have considered only a short time earlier.

These buyers truly believe that renting is the worst outcome, so they will bid furiously in fear. And this is really sad because renting for a while is a far better option than buying the wrong property and/or paying too much.

For all of the bidders I've covered so far, the prime motivation is *winning!* They all want to win for different reasons but the common denominator is that often the value of the property is secondary to the outcome. They are dangerous to take on and it's crucial that you have a clear idea what the property is worth before you bid so that you avoid getting into a bidding war. An arsenal of bidding tactics may not work – sometimes it's better to walk away.

NERVOUS BIDDERS

These guys would also love to buy the property but they are easily spooked. You can usually spot them because they'll have a look of pure fear on their face! They'll often not bid when faced with a dominant opponent. They'll also hold back if nobody else is bidding because they like the reassurance that comes with the knowledge they're not the only interested party. It's a bit of a paradox but that's the psychology of auctions for you.

DUMMY BIDDERS

It's illegal but it doesn't mean it doesn't happen. A small percentage of agents will use dummy bidders when they know they only have one or two interested buyers. Sometimes the owner asks one of their friends to help things along a bit.

There are usually some tell-tale signs. They are often the opening bidder and make that bid a lot quicker than is usual. The auctioneer doesn't usually talk to them much; let's face it, they'll bid without needing to be encouraged. Sometimes the agent walks up to them and actually gives them an instruction.

If it's a slow auction and I suspect there's a dummy bidder, I'll stop bidding and see what happens. Watch the agents go into a tailspin. They *do not* want the dummy to be the highest bidder! They'll come out with all sorts of lines to get me to increase my bid.

Once again, if you know what the property is worth and you have set your maximum bid, it's less of an issue if there is a dummy bidder at the auction. My advice is not to compete with them. Let the agent know you suspect that other bidder is not legitimate but that you still want to buy the property. You can quietly tell them that in the middle of the auction. If it's a dummy bidder, the agent will stop them from bidding any more. If it's a real buyer, you'll see that they keep bidding and you'll need to compete if the price is still within your limit.

CASE STUDY

A sales agent named Theresa told me this one. She took a property to auction and was expecting two buyers to turn up. Now, this was in Melbourne, where bidders don't need to register. When a third person, whom she'd never seen before, started bidding, she was taken by surprise. This bidder was pretty aggressive and Theresa was very happy to see the price rising steadily. Then bidding stalled just short of the reserve price and the unknown buyer was holding the highest bid. Theresa spoke to her vendor to see if he'd lower the reserve price in the hope that would kick off the bidding again. At that point the owner sheepishly confessed that the highest bidder was actually his mate and not a real buyer. You can imagine how furious Theresa was. She passed the property in. The highest bidder vanished and she was left to negotiate with the second highest bidder who subsequently bought the property a few days later for less than he bid up to on the day.

BUYER'S AGENTS

With increasing awareness, there are more of us around, so it's not unlikely to find you're up against a buyer's agent at auction. Like any industry, you'll find there are great ones and woeful ones. There are numerous benefits to using a buyer's agent to bid for you at auction and the most obvious is that you are getting a professional to do the job and take the emotion out of it. I don't recommend engaging a buyer's agent simply to bid, however, because the devil is in the detail! The most value is gained through having advice on the actual calibre of the property, what it is worth (i.e. what your maximum bid should be) and the best strategy. When you engage a professional early in the campaign, you'll be able to properly consider whether it would be better to try to buy it prior to auction rather than wait and bid at auction.

When you are being advised by a buyer's agent (as distinct from having a buyer's agent simply bidding at auction for you) you are going to have a much greater chance of success while also limiting the possibility of paying too much.

If you find yourself bidding against a buyer's agent, don't let them distract you or put you off your game. Stick to your plan and stick to your limit. Watch the other bidders; in particular, watch who the buyer's agent is watching.

Most of the time they'll have a budget and they'll stick to it at the auction. You can expect them to be confident and you shouldn't be able to read into any of their actions. If they have their client with them, watch the client as they'll be the one to give signs that they're close to their limit.

GETTING SOMEONE ELSE TO BID FOR YOU

If you find that auctions scare the pants off you, or if you can't trust yourself to stick to a limit, then it's probably a good idea to get some-body else to bid for you. Often a confident friend or family member is happy to volunteer. This can be a good thing if they can be trusted to keep a level head.

Be careful of people who say they are good at bidding, though. They often have absolutely no idea of what it takes to be a good bidder. They may think that being aggressive is the only trait they need. What you need is someone who is respectful of the important milestone you are taking.

The most important thing here is that you instruct them properly. You need to know in advance of the auction what your maximum bid is going to be. Make sure you have really pushed yourself to your maximum comfort level for that property before setting your limit. There's no point having regrets after the auction as you won't get a second chance.

YOUR GAMEPLAN: WHAT DO YOU DO WHEN ...?

THE AUCTIONEER ASKS FOR AN OPENING BID?

When the auctioneer finishes their preamble, they'll ask for an opening bid. There's usually silence, followed by a well-rehearsed joke to release the tension. And then what?

There's nothing wrong with being the first bidder. This goes against conventional wisdom, which is not to bid until the property is called 'on the market.' You have a better chance of controlling the auction if you start it with a strategic bid. But that is the key – this opportunity must not be wasted.

When there are a lot of other bidders (of course, this is easier to work out in states where bidders have to register) you can use this opportunity to take control by making a strong bid, higher than the agent's quoted guide.

When there are few other bidders (one or two) you can use the opening bid to create doubt by making a low bid. Not ridiculously low, but around 10 percent less than the agent's guide price.

If you want to test the mood in the room, don't make the first bid. Hang back and observe others before you decide on your bidding tactics.

YOU'RE THE ONLY BIDDER?

There are a few ways this can pan out. A deal-focussed agent might take you aside before the auction commences and explain to you that you are the only one likely to bid. If they've built up a relationship with you over the course of the campaign, they'll suggest how this can play out.

A less sophisticated agent will run the auction the same way they would with ten bidders. You'll only realise that you are the only interested party when nobody else raises their hand.

Now, it's an odd thing, as much as we dislike the idea of competing at auction, it seems that we hate the feeling of being the only bidder even more. It's important to remember that you went to the auction to buy the property, you've done your due diligence and really thought about the price you're prepared to pay. You're ready. Now is not the time to second-guess yourself.

You make the first bid, then the agent comes up to you and asks you to increase it. Or maybe the auctioneer responds with a vendor's bid. Either way, what's probably going through your head is *I don't want to look stupid. I'm not going to bid against myself.*

This concept of 'bidding against yourself' is an interesting one. More than once I have heard the highest bidder at an auction say 'I am not going to bid against myself' when the agent quietly informs them that they are under reserve price and suggests an increase. Sometimes that is fair enough: such as when bidding has been competitive and the vendor's reserve is too high. But other times the agent knows that the price reached during a flat auction could be exceeded if the property stays on the market for another week or two at an advertised price. Under these circumstances you wouldn't be 'bidding against yourself', you'd be negotiating.

You have two options here. You could negotiate while the auction is still in progress. The agent will come to you, and you'll increase your offer. They'll then go back to the vendor, who will accept it or reject it and maybe give a counter-offer. This toing and froing can go on for some time and there will be a lot of pressure on you. I recommend asking, 'What price will they sell it for?' If you don't get a straight (and acceptable) answer, then let the agent know you're happy to let it pass in and continue negotiating afterwards.

If the agent says something like 'the owner is prepared to take a lower figure now but their price will go up after the auction', you have my permission to laugh in their face. I hate that line. It's ridiculous to think that the property will be worth more on Monday than it is on the preceding Saturday.

THE AUCTIONEER REFUSES YOUR BID?

The auctioneer will have a game plan and if your bid is too low, they'll reject it. You can either increase it to give them what they want or you can hang back and see how the bidding unfolds. If nobody else bids, they'll come back to you.

If you know what the property is worth and make a really low bid that falls flat, you can then have the confidence to increase your bid. But if you have no idea what it is really worth you will not know what to do.

If you are nowhere near market value and there are no other bids, the auctioneer will pass the property in. The agent and owner will simply wait till another buyer is found who will pay market price.

YOU CAN SEE THE OTHER BIDDERS ARE OVER THEIR LIMIT?

Most bidders give clear signals when they are at or beyond their comfort level. They may look at their partner for the first time since the auction started, they may whisper to their partner and look up and make a $1,000 bid, they may shake their head at the auctioneer and then come back in with a desperate bid.

I've seen many instances when a few buyers were in this state and hesitant thousand dollar bids pushed the price further than anybody expected. In one auction, these bids added an additional hundred thousand dollars to the price! This is the sort of momentum auctioneers strive to achieve. Yet one brave, decisive bid could probably have shut it down.

You can only bid confidently and bravely if you know the property's value and you know your limit. When faced with buyers who are not as well prepared as you are and you know they are second-guessing themselves, don't be afraid to scare them off.

THE PROPERTY PASSES IN?

Make the agent aware that you are not playing games. You'd like to continue negotiating but prefer to do so without the pressure of the auctioneer and crowd.

You need to know that the highest bidder's right to exclusive post-auction negotiation is only a courtesy. The agent and vendor are able to negotiate with any interested party once the property has passed in. They will usually offer the highest bidder the first right of refusal, however there may be other parties suddenly making offers. By leaving the negotiations until after the property has passed in, some vendors harden their stance and a good buying opportunity could pass you by.

Increasing your bid after an auction isn't always a silly thing to do, particularly if you know that you are still way short of a fair price. By all means, try for a bargain and take advantage of being in the box seat. But keep in mind that if you are way off the mark, and the owner does have a realistic price expectation, in all likelihood, they will find another buyer before too long.

SNEAKY TACTICS THE AUCTIONEER WILL USE TO GET YOU TO BID MORE

There are some auctioneers who are at the top of their game and are very skilled at being able to influence your bidding.

The first thing they will try to do is make you (and every other buyer) feel like you have a chance of owning the property. It's only then that you are likely to bid and it is also that belief that will keep you bidding.

What they really want to do is get as many hands in the air as possible and create momentum. When buyers are bidding, when there's a rhythm to it, the bids keep coming and the auctioneer's job is to coax things along until every last dollar has been extracted.

Of course, auctions don't always go to plan and an accomplished auctioneer has a series of tricks and tools that they will use to entice you to bid.

A SENSE OF URGENCY

One of the reasons that most auctioneers don't make an announcement when the reserve price has been met is that they want you to feel like it could sell at any price. They'll basically call your bluff so that you'll bid.

Many auctioneers will call the property three times ('going once, going twice, going three times ...') regularly during the auction because they want to spur bidders into action. If you haven't bid yet and you think it's going to be sold at less than your budget, of course you're going to put your hand up.

To add increased emphasis, you'll often see them raise their gavel (or a rolled-up contract) and let it hover in the air. It's a brave buyer who can call an auctioneer's bluff under that pressure.

BODY LANGUAGE

Auctioneers can be extremely skilled at watching all the non-verbal signs that you give away. Facial expressions, nervous whispered conversations, your hand moving towards your bidding card or paddle ...

If they see that one buyer is struggling and you are looking stronger, they'll encourage you and use the power of suggestion to prise a higher bid out of you. They might say, 'Look, one more bid might buy it. Make it a strong one, round it up ...'

If they see you are starting to waver, some auctioneers will try to override your internal voice of indecision by talking more and speaking directly to you. They might say, 'You've been looking for a long time, do you really want to go back to the drawing board when you've come this far?'

If they see two buyers are both near the end of their respective runs, they'll encourage them both to place smaller bids in order to stay in the game.

WHEN IS IT 'ON THE MARKET'?

Despite the fact that you will rarely hear the words 'on the market', nearly every auctioneer will make it very clear when it really is about to be sold. They will say something like 'make no mistake, we are selling'. Or perhaps you have seen the selling agent go inside the property and confer with the owners. Then they come out and whisper to the auctioneer, following which they might say, 'My vendor's instructions are clear, the property is about to be sold.'

They are *not* bluffing you when this happens.

The bottom line is that if you don't bid, you won't buy. As I've said so many times before, set your limit before you go to auction and you'll run your own race and be less likely to be influenced by the auctioneer.

If you'd like to learn some of these techniques straight from the auctioneer's mouth, there are four episodes of *The Elephant in the Room* property podcast you should listen to. You'll find them on www. getauctionready.com.au/bonus.

BIDDER MISTAKES TO AVOID

PAY ATTENTION

There are a lot of mistakes that buyers can make at auction through not paying attention. Trying to be too clever or simply being distracted and stressed can lead to you either paying more than you need to or missing out altogether.

BID BEFORE THE HAMMER FALLS

It doesn't occur often but I have seen this happen. A bidder waits too long to bid. The auctioneer calls the property three times, the gavel falls and then the buyer puts their hand up and says 'one million'...

Maybe they've been told that they shouldn't bid until they hear the words 'it's on the market.' Maybe they've zoned out. Maybe they are arrogant and wanted to prove a point.

Whatever the reason, they just missed out on the property. You must bid before the hammer falls. The auctioneer cannot accept bids after the property has sold.

ACCIDENTALLY BIDDING AGAINST YOURSELF

I've seen the highest bidder at auction panic and increase their bid a split second before the property is sold – to them! In one instance the auctioneer very generously allowed the buyer to retract that final bid and they purchased it at their next highest bid. I've seen other auctioneers take that increased bid and the buyer had to pay more.

When you are bidding, you must pay attention to who the bid is with and how much that bid is. Stay focussed!

NUMERICALLY CHALLENGED

Once the bidding goes beyond a million dollars, it can be challenging to keep up with the numbers. I've seen and heard buyers bid 'one point two' when they really mean 'one million and twenty'. It happens a lot more often than you'd imagine.

My tip here is to spell it out. Don't use shorthand. 'One point two' means 'one million and two hundred thousand'. If you really meant 'one point zero two', you're offering $180,000 more than you thought you were.

CASE STUDY

I heard a story about an auction for a property that sold for $6,750,000. You'd imagine that anybody bidding on a property worth that much would be able to keep track of the numbers, but not this guy. The highest bidder paused after a run of spirited bidding. He asked the auctioneer to confirm where the bid was at. The auctioneer advised him, '6.75 million', to which he responded, 'No, 5.75 million.' The auctioneer apparently quickly realised that this buyer had lost track of which million he was in. The auctioneer counted three times and dropped the hammer. The property sold to the highest bidder for a million dollars more than he thought he'd bid.

Sometimes auctioneers are also numerically challenged. I once bought a property for a client for less than we'd bid because the auctioneer had lost track of what price had been reached.

If it helps, write down the bids as they happen and you can ask the auctioneer at any point during the auction to confirm what the highest bid is. Bids can come fast and furious and you need to be prepared for this.

CHAPTER 9

AFTER THE AUCTION

SUCCESS! THE PROPERTY IS YOURS

You're the highest bidder! The property has been knocked down to you! Now what?

You'll be required to sign the contract and pay your deposit immediately. The agent will guide you here.

Advise your solicitor/conveyancer and your mortgage broker/bank manager as soon as possible that you've purchased a property and what the settlement date will be. They'll each let you know what's required of you next.

If you have just bought a new home, you'll have a lot to get organised. If you're renting, you'll need to give your property manager notice to vacate. If you need to sell, you'd better let your chosen agent know.

If you've bought the property as an investment, appoint a property manager as soon as possible and see what they can do to get the property leased quickly. I recommend also letting your accountant know so that you can get the financial side of things set up in the most advantageous way.

Congratulations! You don't need to read the rest of this book.

WHAT HAPPENS IF IT PASSED IN?

If the vendor is holding out for too much money, then it is worth letting the property pass in. This is one reason why it's so important to know your walk-away price before the auction. You could let another buyer pay more and get the property, or you could battle it out with the owner. When the property passes in, we usually try to negotiate a deal immediately afterwards, but only if the ultimate price represents good value. If you really want it and they are prepared to sell it for less than or equal to your upper limit, then buy it.

If you can't reach agreement on price the agent will keep you in the loop. You may still have the opportunity to buy the property within your budget in the days and weeks that follow.

Remember that the best way for the owner to sell unconditionally is at the auction and they may need to give you a cooling off period if you strike a deal at a later date. This is to your advantage – use it if you're continuing negotiations on the day of auction.

CASE STUDY

I once bid on a house for a client where there were seven registered bidders and strong competition. I was astounded to see that as the price climbed, the auctioneer motioned to the agent to speak to the vendor about the reserve price. As it turned out, the reserve was ridiculously high. The agent hadn't prepared any of the buyers for this and neither had she managed to get her vendor in the right mindset to sell.

The buyers started to get suspicious and then the mood of the auction changed. Everybody stopped bidding. We weren't the highest bidder. I'd stopped bidding as soon as I realised that the reserve price wasn't going to be met. There was no point inflating the price under those circumstances.

Three weeks later, the owner decided to meet the market and lower their asking price. By this stage, a couple of the other buyers had bought elsewhere and others had talked themselves out of the property. We bought it for our clients for $27,000 less than the highest bid.

BUYERS BEWARE: THE MOST VULNERABLE BUYER IS THE ONE WHO JUST MISSED OUT AT AUCTION

Have you ever met someone who married on the rebound? It's a messy situation and once they realise what's happened their choice is either to make the best of it or get out. The same thing can happen with house hunters after they miss out on a home they really wanted. It's a surprisingly common mistake and one that costs a lot of money to fix.

When you are suffering the disappointment of missing out on your dream home (as so often happens in auction-oriented areas), you are at your most vulnerable.

So often we seek to immediately dull the pain of a loss. But if you try to do so by leaping into a desperate purchase you may just find that the long-term grief is so much harder to bear. You don't want the pain to wear off only to realise that you have committed to buying a property that is less than ideal. There is too much at stake to use emotion as your only decision-making tool.

CASE STUDY

I saw a young man bidding at auction once. It was heartbreaking because by rights he should have bought the house. It was his timid, uncertain bidding that brought him undone in the face of a much more confident bidder.

After the auction I spoke with him and his wife, who had been standing in the wings with their baby. They were desperate to buy a family home and devastated at missing out.

Two weeks later the house across the road went to auction. They'd seen it and told me they weren't interested. I could understand why as it wasn't at all family-friendly. I spoke to them the afternoon before the auction for this second house and his wife told me they planned to go to the auction but assured me that they wouldn't bid.

However, I knew the selling agent and I was pretty sure she wouldn't let them off the hook. Sure enough, they registered and bid. They hadn't done a building and pest inspection, nor did they get the contract reviewed. They bought the property for only $15,000 less than the one they missed out on two weeks earlier. It was nowhere near as good.

What many buyers don't realise is that if you have decided to sell before you buy, you are also susceptible to the same pressure immediately after selling. This is usually because we resist the idea of renting – who wouldn't want to avoid a double move, after all?

Beware: this is the time you need to be more critical than ever! Try the helicopter approach and look at the big picture. Remember why you wanted to move in the first place and revise your property requirements. Organise your checklist so that your must-haves are at the top of the list. Review what you are prepared to compromise on before you inspect the next property. Now be honest with yourself: are you buying out of fear or because this is the right property for you?

Please allow yourself time to find the right property for you. Act in haste, repent at leisure.

GETTING BACK ON THE HORSE

It's tough when you miss out on a property you really want. But there are worse things than missing out. Paying too much is one and buying the wrong property is another. These are things that rebound buyers do.

Some buyers react to being beaten at a competitive auction by diving for cover. They take a long time to lick their wounds and recover from such a brutal reminder of how difficult it can be to buy their dream home (or any home for that matter!). And when they resurface, they often make the very same mistake they made this first time: falling for a property that everybody else seems to want and being ill-prepared.

I'm here to encourage you to keep pressing on. Remember why you wanted to buy a property in the first place and don't give up hope.

The trick is to stay in the market: persist and educate yourself on what constitutes a good property and what prices are reasonable. Believe it or not there are good buying opportunities out there, but you have to be active in the market in order to find them – so just don't give up!

If your expectations are out of alignment with the market, face up to it and be realistic about what you can get for your money. Don't fall into the wishful-thinking trap that a low auction price guide can lure you into.

Here's another trap to avoid: after missing out at auction some buyers decide they will never again look at an auction property. This means that they cut down their chances of finding a quality property as quite often most of the good ones go to auction.

If you've fallen foul of underquoting, don't tar all real estate agents with the same brush and end up being rude and dismissive to them. This is the way to ensure you're given no favours and it will reduce your chances of getting any information that will help you to be the eventual buyer.

And don't be one of those bitter and twisted would-be buyers who constantly talk about the impending market crash as a way of justifying why you haven't bought a home.

Now, don't misunderstand me, it can be tough out there and auctions are not easy to master. After every disappointment it's important to dust yourself off, learn the lessons you need and leave the negative reactions behind. Get back on the horse, apply everything you've learnt in this book and GET AUCTION READY!

GLOSSARY

66W Certificate

In NSW the only way a buyer can waive the cooling off period on a contract (except when buying at auction) is to have their solicitor or conveyancer provide a 66W Certificate. They issue this after they have explained the contract to their client and the risks of proceeding without a cooling off period.

Buyer's agent

A buyer's agent, or buyer's advocate as often referred to in Victoria, is a real estate agent who acts for buyers instead of sellers. Unfortunately the term is not (yet) regulated, so anybody can effectively call themselves a buyer's agent, so be careful. A true buyer's agent will be paid by the buyer for their services and exclusively work for that buyer.

Capital growth

In simple terms, this is the amount that your property increased in value since you bought it.

Capital gains

When your accountant works out your capital gain, they'll subtract from the capital growth figure the costs associated with purchasing, borrowing, renovating and selling the property.

Capital gains tax (CGT)

If your property is your principal place of residence (i.e. you live in it and have always lived in it since purchase) then you won't have to pay tax on the capital gain when you sell. If, however, your property is an investment property, or has been for a period of time, then you will need to pay some tax. It's complicated, so keep all records from purchase onwards and engage a good accountant.

Capital gains tax concession

Property investors in Australia currently get a 50 percent CGT discount. This means that after your accountant has calculated the CGT, you only have to pay tax on half of that figure. Be aware that this might change at some point in the future, as the ALP were aiming to do if they won the 2019 federal election.

Conveyancer

You'll need to engage a lawyer or conveyancer to review the contract when you buy a property. A conveyancer is different to a lawyer in that they ONLY work on property matters. They're often less expensive than a lawyer too. But this doesn't mean that they aren't as good. We'd take an experienced conveyancer every day over a lawyer who doesn't specialise in property.

Equity

This is the difference between what the property is worth and how much you owe the bank. It's what you actually own.

Lenders mortgage insurance (LMI)

This is an insurance policy that covers the bank in the event that you default on your loan. Most lenders require you to pay the premium if your deposit is less than 20 percent.

Negative gearing

It's a tax concession that allows an investor to get a tax deduction for losses.

Say you're a property investor who's out of pocket $1,000 a month because the rent doesn't cover the interest on your mortgage after accounting for depreciation and costs. You could then claim $12,000 a year against your tax.

Rentvesting

A fairly new term that describes when somebody chooses to rent where they live and buy a more affordable investment property that's either smaller than they need or in a less expensive location.

Selling agent

A real estate agent who is engaged by an owner to sell their home.

Stamp duty

This is a state based tax on property transactions. The exact amount varies from state to state.

ABOUT THE AUTHOR

With so many property 'experts' out there, you can cut through all the noise with this book as it's been written by one of Australia's most recognisable property buyers. Veronica Morgan has bid at hundreds of auctions around Australia – both on and off TV.

Veronica is probably best known for her role as co-host of *Location Location Location Australia* and *Relocation Relocation Australia* on Foxtel's The Lifestyle Channel. She is also a Licensed Real Estate Agent, principal of Sydney based Good Deeds Property Buyers and co-founder of Home Buyer Academy. Veronica understands the other side of the equation too, having commenced her property career as a sales agent back in 2000. She became one of her area's leading agents and excelled in managing auction campaigns over a six-year sales career. Veronica was a regular guest co-host on the Your Money *Auction Day* program and also co-hosts *The Elephant in the Room* property podcast, where she interviews auctioneers, agents and other industry professionals in order to uncover their tricks of the trade.

www.ingramcontent.com/pod-product-compliance
Lightning Source LLC
Chambersburg PA
CBHW071233210326
41597CB00016B/2029